Grazia Ietto Gillies was born in Calabria in 1939 and spent the first ten years of her life in Delianuova, a small town in the Aspromonte mountains. She moved to Rome with her family in 1950 and has lived in London since 1971. She has worked and published as an academic economist.

https://graziaiettogillies.wordpress.com.

'From the goat bells of Calabria to the traffic of South London, from a classroom in a dressmaker's house to lecturing at a metropolitan university, and from childhood to adulthood, Grazia Ietto Gillies takes the reader on an enchanting journey involving memory and her Mamma's cooking. The passage of time and the timelessness of Italian recipes make this an extraordinary tale of displacement, discontinuity and, ultimately, reconnection. If music be the food of love, then it is the love of food that makes this memoir sing.'
Nick Barlay, author of *Scattered Ghosts: One Family's Survival through War, Holocaust and Revolution*

'In *By the Olive Groves*, Grazia Ietto Gillies has written a testament to the creative power of the Mediterranean kitchen. A daughter's lifelong appreciation for Mamma Giulia's ingenuity and good taste lies at the heart of this story of one family's rise from the hard mountains of Calabria to Roman postwar prosperity. Rich in characters, memories and, above all, recipes, this evocative memoir is also a guide to the history and cuisine of a region.'
Catherine Davidson, author of *The Priest Fainted*

'If you have ever been enchanted by southern Italy; if you have left the house of childhood, but often return there in imagination; if you think cooking is an important part of life; or if you consider economics and poetics to be closely related: then you must read this book. Travel with Grazia Ietto Gillies across the horseshoe-shaped high street of Delianuova in Calabria, from her house (perfumed by her mother's cooking) to those of her cousins, then down the slopes to Reggio Calabria, facing Sicily and the straits of Scylla and Charybdis. Warmly and thoughtfully evoking her childhood, she brings the town and its environs, history and inhabitants to life with her green-golden pen, the colour of sunlight filtering through an olive leaf.'
Emily Grosholz, poet, philosopher and Advisory Editor, *The Hudson Review*

GRAZIA IETTO GILLIES

By the Olive Groves

A Calabrian Childhood

I.B. TAURIS

LONDON · NEW YORK

Published in 2017 by
I.B.Tauris & Co. Ltd
London • New York
www.ibtauris.com

ISBN: 978 1 78453 546 9
eISBN: 978 1 78672 129 7
ePDF: 978 1 78673 129 6

A full CIP record for this book is available from the British Library
A full CIP record is available from the Library of Congress

Library of Congress Catalog Card Number: available

Typeset in Goudy Old Style by A. & D. Worthington, Newmarket
Printed and bound in Sweden by ScanBook AB

To the memory of my parents
and
for their great-grandchildren

Contents

Illustrations

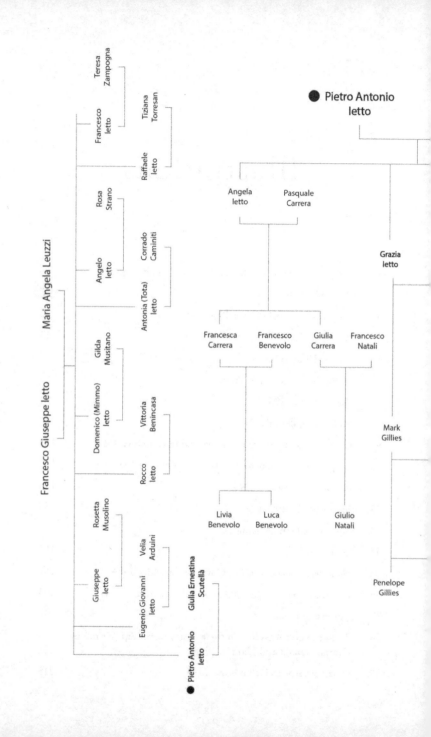

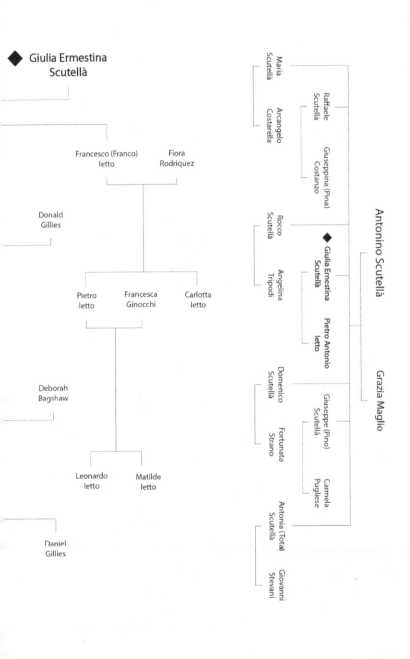

Acknowledgements

Many family and friends have read successive drafts of this memoir and offered welcome suggestions. My mother-in-law, Katharine Ross Gillies, read it in 2006, in her 95th year, and gave enthusiastic encouragement to proceed further and publish it and to include photographs. Sadly she passed away in her 98th year, having retained her mental power and interest in literature almost to the last. Francesco Abbate and Donatella Badin Abbate read a version in 2007 and gave encouraging and useful comments. Simonetta Agnello Hornby read it in 2009 and offered welcome advice. A chance encounter led to the first person outside the family and friends circle reading it in 2011 and offering much needed encouragement. Howard Davies's kind, competent and generous comments gave me the resolve to seek publication. Emily Grosholz's very positive comments in 2011 led to much improvement and further resolve. She also helped to tidy up the final draft.

I am also grateful to Emily for her introduction to the Upper Wimpole Street Literary Salon organized by Sarah Glazer. Participation in their stimulating meetings increased my desire to continue the project. Shelley Weiner read it in 2012 and offered encouraging comments and very useful advice on the structure. The revised 2013 version was read by my friend and economist colleague Marion Frenz who was also very encouraging. Alix Kirsta has given me much needed advice on navigating through the confusing world of agents and publishers and on preparing material for them. Her friend Nick Barlay was very helpful in suggesting that I approach Tatiana Wilde at I.B.Tauris. Another fortuitous encounter led to Polly Coles reading it and offering very perceptive comments.

My uncle Angelo Ietto provided information on my paternal great grandfather, and my cousin Nino Scutellà on my maternal great grandfather. Sadly Nino died in 2015. My cousins Grazia and Giuseppina Stevani have supplied a photograph of their mother, Tota Scutellà; my cousin Daniela Caminiti has given me valuable information and reading material about Delianuova; and Raffaele Leuzzi has provided me with digital copies of photos of Delianuova in the 1940s. My friend Marika Lucisano has kindly provided reading material on Reggio and on 'I bronzi di Riace'. Finn Dean has managed to represent my large extended family as three, simple family trees.

My editor Tatiana Wilde has given encouragement, support and – most relevant for me – has believed in the project from when I first contacted I.B.Tauris. I am grateful to David Campbell for efficiently overseeing the production and to David Worthington for his pleasing design and for dealing well with the copy-editing of a demanding script.

To Donald and Mark I owe much more than gratitude for reading this memoir and offering comments and support. They are the very reason why I have happily settled in Britain. The geographical, cultural and social displacement effect that this has had on me I consider to be the main drive behind my desire – indeed urge – to write the memoir.

Many, many thanks to all of you.

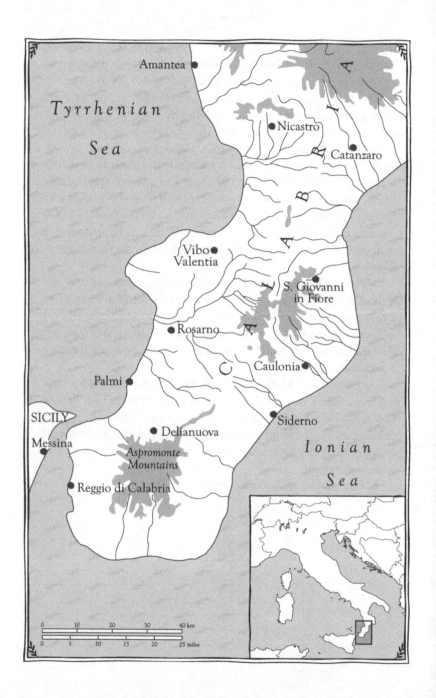

Preface

Who is entitled to write his reminiscences?
Everyone. ...
In order to write one's reminiscences it is not at all necessary to be
a great man, nor a notorious criminal, nor a celebrated artist, nor a
statesman - it is quite enough to be simply a human being, to have
something to tell ...
Alexander Herzen

Delianuova, the small Calabrian town at the heart of this memoir,
is located on a hill slope between the Aspromonte massif on the
inland side and the plain of Gioia Tauro on the Tyrrhenian coast
side. On the inland side the hill leads up to the Piani di Carmelia,
a high-level plain from where a steep ascent takes the determined
visitor up towards Montalto and the Aspromonte peaks. Against
local advice, Norman Douglas walked his way up from Delianuova
to the peaks and then down to Bova on the Ionian coast during
his visit to Calabria in 1911. He walked through groves of chestnuts, beeches, firs and 'long stretches of odorous pines interspersed
with Mediterranean heath (*bruyere*), which here grows to a height
of twelve feet'.

On the Tyrrhenian side the land gradually descends towards
the sea. The traveller is taken through magnificent olive groves.
Planted randomly through the plain and low hill, the trees have
been part of the landscape for centuries. Their large, twisted and
gnarled trunks seem at odds with the tiny, delicate, silvery leaves

springing from their branches. They shimmer and change colour,
playing with the sun and being played with by the wind. Moving
on towards the coast, travellers pass orange, mandarin and lemon
orchards as well as terraces of vines. Occasionally, in dry areas,
the prickly Indian fig plant establishes itself. Near the scattered
sequence of small towns and hamlets, fig trees huddle against
houses for warmth. The hospitality is amply rewarded by their
sweet fruits.

Calabria, surrounded by the Ionian and Tyrrhenian seas, is the
Italian region with the highest length of coast per surface area. It
is also a region in which the terrain reaches very high peaks within
a relatively small space, leaving the inhabitants with little fertile
land. From very early on the sea has been their main resource. It
was also the source of their main threats: incursions by invaders
and pirates. The inhabitants were forced over and over again to
move inland and up the hills and mountains for protection. And
this is how my little town originated.

Delianuova was born from the merger of two villages, Pedavoli
and Paracorio, which still form two *quartieri* and parishes. Originally the two hamlets were established by people escaping from
aggressive sea incursions in the two centuries preceding the first
millennium – Paracorio by refugees from the southern Ionian coast
near Bova. The name is of Greek origin, meaning 'people from
over the mountains'. The refugees belonged to the Greek colony of
Delia, which eventually gave the modern name to my town. They
travelled in the opposite direction to the hard walk taken by Douglas many centuries later.

Pedavoli was established by refugees from Tauriana on the
Tyrrhenian coast. Thus the peoples in the two hamlets originated from two different coastal areas and two, opposite sides
of the Aspromonte mountain: the steeply ascending side that
overlooks the Tyrrhenian and the more gentle side descending
towards the Ionian Sea. The two villages were brought closer
together by a natural disaster. The earthquake of 1783 destroyed
Paracorio and led to its reconstruction near Pedavoli, on the
present site. The two hamlets merged into a new town which
was officially established as an independent administrative entity

in 1878 following the unification of Italy in 1861.

The union of the two hamlets started an organic process of expansion as houses were built huddled together for protection. It led to the development of Delianuova in a horseshoe pattern marked by its main street, Corso Umberto. The central part of the horseshoe sits on the hillside and the two sides descend separately towards the valley. Uncontrolled building in the last few decades make it now difficult to identify the old pattern. On both sides of the corso smaller streets spread up the hill and down the valley. They lead to a myriad of other paths, sometimes connected, sometimes keeping their independence. On the outskirts of the town there are several rivulets and small cascades. Geographic milestones in the town consisted of the two secular pine trees towards the ends of the central side of the horseshoe. Sad, historical milestones are the earthquakes of 1894, 1905 and, particularly, the 1908 one.

Delianuova is some 70km away from Reggio Calabria, the capital of the province and the largest local town. Reggio lies on the south-west coast of the mainland opposite Messina, on the eastern side of Sicily. It was established by the Greeks – as Rheghion – in the eighth century BC. There followed similar settlements in Locri, Sibari and Crotone, all along the Ionian Sea. Sibari's riches and indulgent lifestyle proved its downfall: the people from Crotone sacked and destroyed it in 510 BC. Many centuries later, it was a local bishop who destroyed the best testimony of Greek civilization in the town. He sacked the Crotone Greek Temple in search of stone and marble to build his luxurious palace. George Gissing's pain and anger at this act of archeological vandalism is almost palpable in his *By the Ionian Sea*.

Calabria's history is one of a sequence of invasions, destructions and reconstructions, as is most of Italy's. The local population, the Brutii, were invaded by Greek colonists. The Greeks were gradually displaced by the Romans who in turn were forced out by the Goths and the Byzantines. Other peoples from the north had a go and stayed for centuries: from the Longobards to the Normans to the Suevians. The French and the Spaniards ruled in centuries nearer ours. Eventually in 1861 Calabria became part of a united Italy, a process that many saw as one more conquest, this time from the king of Piedmont in northern Italy. His troops fought and wounded Garibaldi in a famous battle on the Aspromonte plain in 1860. The hero of the Italian Risorgimento handed over his southern conquests to the king of Piedmont, soon to become king of Italy. He also handed over his dream of an Italian republic. That dream was realized in 1946 following the fall of the fascist regime and the end of World War II. Many Italians, including my parents, exercised enthusiastically their newly won right to vote. They rejected the monarchy, which they saw as having supported Mussolini.

International and national events did not always spare this remote town. Pedavoli was the site of an uprising and battle against the Bourbons in 1847, just at the time when the British landscape painter and traveller Edward Lear was passing through. He was recording Calabria in drawings and words, looking at it through the romantic spectacles of the time. The revolutionary events forced him to shelve his plan to go through the northern part of Calabria and cut short his visit.

During the early years of these reminiscences Delianuova had some 6,000 inhabitants. Those war and post-World War II years were hard for my family. They were also among the worse experienced by the town in the twentieth century in terms of economic and social conditions. In 1955 the infant mortality rate in Calabria was over 62 per 1,000 live births. In the Delianuova of 1951 almost a third of the population was illiterate and only 40 per cent had primary education. University degrees were held by only 20 people, of which two were women. Large migrations abroad and to the north of Italy in search of employment later led to a decline in the resident population which now stands at around 3,500.

The town architecture shows clear signs of more prosperous times, at least for part of the population, in the two preceding centuries. The town has two large and beautiful churches in its two parishes. The Paracorio church - Chiesa Maria SS Assunta - was rebuilt after the earthquake of 1894. The Pedavoli church - Chiesa di San Nicola - dates back to the seventeenth century with considerable rebuilding in the eighteenth and nineteenth centuries. Both have interesting works from local, past and more recent artists. Other small churches, including some private ones, are no longer used for religious purposes. Scattered around Delianuova's corso are also some very large houses with impressive portals carved in the local green stone, the *pietra verde*. Most of these large mansions were built or rebuilt in the nineteenth century after the destructions of the 1783 quake.

The last few decades have seen a cultural revival on the back of economic improvements. Delianuova now has an excellent youth orchestra as well as a bookshop and publishing company specializing in local history and literature. But social problems, old and new, still mar its fabric.

I was born in October 1939 and began school in 1945. In 1950 I moved to Rome with my family, retaining close contacts with Delianuova. My sister, brother and I used to spend our summer vacations in Delianuova well into our teens, but these visits became less frequent as I grew up. My interests shifted towards study, a career as an academic economist - first in Italy and then in Britain - and private life. I married Donald, a British philosopher of science and mathematics, in 1971 and our son Mark was born in 1975.

Though I only lived in Delianuova for the first ten years of my life, in my thoughts and emotional life I never left it. Moreover the society we came from had a lasting impact on my Italian family. In the last few decades I have visited Delianuova very often through my imagination and memories but rarely in person. This separation may explain why the memories of an earlier society have remained so vivid. They have not been affected by the economic, social and cultural changes that have taken place in Delianuova in the last few decades.

Readers may wonder why - if I was and still am so attached to and affected by my early life in Delianuova - I have not been back there more often. I might be tempted to say that as my parents and siblings were in Rome I saw no need to visit the town. The truth is more complex and has to do with my family's contradictory feelings and attitudes towards Delianuova and its people. We talked endlessly about them and yet we felt a sense of fear and hostility towards them.

Memories are multidimensional as well as self-selecting. This is reflected in this book. There are, however, two themes that run through this memoir: the impact that our little Calabrian town and its society had on me and my family; and food. Food played a vital role in our family life and culture and my mother was at the heart of it. She was an excellent provider of family meals. Her cooking is thus an important part of this book. All but three chapters end with Mamma's recipes. They feature her Calabrian style of cooking based on vegetables, pasta dishes and – always – olive oil. 'Grazia, how can you cook a decent meal if you do not have good olive oil in London?' Calm and serene, yet strong willed and determined, she would spend the whole morning in her kitchen. Whenever I approached her little culinary domain, I was welcomed by the perfume of cooking peppers, beans, aubergines, artichokes and courgettes. Their colours were the real decoration in her kitchen, which was simple and lacking modern appliances.

Mamma's cooking was of the type now identified as 'Mediterranean cuisine'. It involves no butter, very little dairy produce and little meat. This was not by choice but due to the availability of local ingredients. It so happens that this is the type of food now considered best by the healthcare community. In fact, the Calabrian town of Nicotera – together with the island of Crete – was chosen by Ancel Keys for his 1957 research into diet. This American medical researcher was at the time planning a very large and ground-breaking study of the effects of diet on cholesterol levels and heart disease.

The vast majority of Mamma's recipes are very easy to cook as well as inexpensive. The last 20 years have seen great changes in the range of food available in developed countries and I can now buy most of the necessary ingredients in my London supermarket. They are not as good as the original Calabrese ones, freshly available when I was a child, but they are good enough to make excellent and healthy meals. Through the years I have developed my own version of some of Mamma's recipes to fit in with the availability of ingredients and with the more limited time at my disposal. My approach to cooking and to Mamma's recipes is that anyone can do it. Cooking is mainly common sense and part of everyday family life. Do not aim for perfection but for healthy, simple, tasty meals. If your dish is not quite as good as you expected, well, it will be better next time. I invite readers to try some of my mother's recipes and to develop versions to suit their families.

This memoir is structured into three parts. Part I presents scenes and anecdotes from my early years in Delianuova and touches on various aspects of social and family life in this remote, under-developed and child-friendly environment. Parts II and III are about the impact that Delianuova had on my later life and on that of my family. Part II relates to our life in Rome, where I grew into a young woman. Part III traces episodes of my life in Britain which were affected by my Calabrian childhood.

The book is based on my recollections. The anecdotes are as accurate as my memory, and the conversations must be read as expressions of the general thrust rather than as records of exact wordings.

PART I
A CHILDHOOD OF LOVE AND OLIVE OIL

1

The milkman and his goats deliver

'Omai convien che tu cosi' ti spoltre'
disse il maestro, che', seggendo in piuma,
in fama non si vien, ne' sotto coltre'

'Now must thou cast off all sloth,' said the master
'for sitting on down or under blankets none comes to fame, ...'
Dante Alighieri

'*Ooh, ferma, veni ccah!*' (Ooh, stop, come here!)

Blah, blah, blah. Ndlon, ndlon, ndlon.

The shouting of 'Ntoni, the bleating of his goats and the clanging of their bells reach me as distant muffled sounds while I struggle to continue my sleep. The struggle is lost as the mattress shakes and my sister jumps out of our shared bed on to our shared chamber pot. Angela, one year older than me, has beaten me to it as usual. The tinkle of her pee into the china pot does not help. Legs tight. I must not let go. The last time I wet myself she called me a baby who needs nappies. The thought is still painful long after the event.

As the younger of the two, I sleep on the side of the bed against the wall. This gives me the advantage of being very close to the window. On cold winter mornings the sight of icicles with their elongated, rugged shapes feeds my fantasies of magic castles, white knights and beautiful damsels for days on end. This morning the attraction is 'Ntoni and his two goats who deliver milk to us. One of the two goats is very small, its coat a silky brown. Its sweet face turns towards me before it decides to wander off. I giggle at its independent spirit as much as at the angry and totally ignored commands it elicits from 'Ntoni.

Soon enough my mother is with them and I see the milk frothing from the udder of the big goat into her pan, under the expert direction of 'Ntoni's hand. But it all ends too quickly. She hands over some coins, smiles and exchanges a few words with taciturn 'Ntoni. She then picks up her pan and a small ricotta cheese and heads back inside. As I take my turn on the pot, I hear Mamma coming up the stairs. She will help us to wash and dress before returning to her kitchen. Then her complaints start.

'Oh that appalling cheat! He has filled my pan with froth again!'

These were the years immediately after World War II. The men who survived it were back but their earnings were low and provisions scarce. Mamma often supplemented the goats' milk with barley coffee to make a decent breakfast for us. On the mornings when 'Ntoni did not appear - for reasons known only to himself according to Mamma - we would have barley coffee only. Into the large bowls filled with steaming liquid we dipped strong, wholemeal bread. Sometimes it was *biscotto di pane*, bread rusk. When crumbled into the hot milky mixture it made a delicious soft meal for us. Another of my favourite dips was sweet biscuits made by my mother. But this treat was rare. What, unfortunately, was not rare was the spoonful of cod liver oil. She had the spoon with the dreaded oil in one hand and an orange segment in the other, ready to be popped into our mouths and soften the taste of fish oil.

This breakfast routine was for us children only. My father - Pietro - would have left home much earlier. Sometimes he spent the night away. His work on building sites was often in other towns. My mother had her beloved espresso when waking up and some bread with olive oil while preparing and serving our breakfast. My brother Francesco - called Franco in the family - two years younger than me, was not always with us.

Before he reached school age, Franco spent large parts of the day and many nights with Mamma Teresa. We took it for granted

1. 1940. Grazia and Angela suspicious of the photographer

that he should have two mammas: Giulia, our own mother, and Teresa, his wet-nursing mother. Teresa was the same age as Giulia and similarly serene, dependable and determined. She came from a peasant background and lived with her husband, father-in-law and children in one of the poorest areas of Delianuova, i Lazzari. Here semi-naked, dirty children with large bellies and boil-covered legs could be seen playing in puddles. The area is now fully developed.

When Franco was born my mother did not have enough breast milk to nurse him. Teresa, whose baby had just died like another two before, was asked to wet-nurse Franco. This was a common practice at the time. Both Angela and I had also been wet-nursed by different women for short periods. Teresa breastfed Franco for a long period and encouraged him to see her as a second mamma. She became very attached to Franco and always believed that the survival of her own three children born after Franco was due to the fact that she had used her milk to nurse him. The truth may have been the reverse: Franco survived thanks to her milk. My mother considered it normal that there should be such a strong bond between Franco and Teresa. When, years later, Teresa and her family were preparing for emigration to Australia she was heart broken to leave her 'fourth child' behind. She timidly suggested to

2. Franco in 1946

my mother that, if allowed the great privilege to take him with her, she would treat him better than her own children. Giulia understood but declined. She promised to encourage communication between them.

She kept her promise. Letters and phone calls were exchanged for the next 50 years or so. Franco and his family went to visit them and Teresa came back to Italy in the early 1980s, accompanied by a successful granddaughter. On that occasion the two mothers spent a happy day together in Rome. They devoted themselves almost entirely to self-congratulations about their wonderful son, telling each other little anecdotes about his good deeds towards them and other people. On the phone from London, I had a chat with Teresa in Calabrese dialect, followed by a talk with her granddaughter in English. I never remember my mother having anything other than kind words to say about Franco's second mamma.

Teresa proved to be a strong woman of remarkable resilience. Her husband died of tuberculosis only months after she joined him in Australia. Uneducated and with no knowledge of her new country and its language, she managed to bring up her three children honestly and well. She worked hard and guided her two boys and one girl towards suitable jobs. She remained in command of her children and grandchildren almost to the end of her life in 2005, two years after Giulia's death. Exchanges between Franco and Teresa's children and grandchildren have continued.

My brother may have benefited from this extra motherly love not only in emotional terms. Contact with the more street-wise children and nephews of Teresa may have helped him in other ways. He grew up skilled in dealing with people's emotional and social conflicts, in mixing with a variety of social groups and in navigating the practical side of life in small or big towns.

After breakfast, it's time for our hair to be combed and dressed. On the top of my head, two small ribbons are knotted into bows to hold the two sides of my hair. For my sister it is no bow at all or a single large one at one side of her head. This is a daily bone of contention.

'I do not want two bows. They make me look like a baby. Now I am older, I go to school like Angela.'

'Yes, I know, Grazietta; you are a big girl now. But two bows are more becoming to your hair and face. You have such a sweet face. Cheer up, I will have your favourite *pasta e ricotta* for lunch.'

'But you are not grown up like me. You are still very small. So you should have two bows.' Angela's unwelcome addition has me bursting into tears.

Angela often boasted about being grown up, sophisticated and experienced compared to me and Franco. The claim to sophistication had its roots in Angela's belief to be a city girl rather than a country bumpkin like her two siblings. Our birth certificates and school reports were clear evidence of this. They stated that we were born in Delianuova and she was born in Reggio Calabria. In the faraway days of her birth my mother became unwell when she was seven months' pregnant. She was taken in the *carabinieri* car from Delianuova to the Reggio hospital where Angela came into the world. They travelled back to Delianuova after a couple of weeks. She was so small that she travelled in a shoe-box lined with cotton wool. She lived in Delianuova, like the rest of us, till the family moved to Rome.

Her claim to experience was based on age difference. She rubbed it in and, at times, abused her seniority rights and duties. On the whole she was gentle and protective towards me but less so towards our brother whom she accused of all sorts of misdemeanours. The accusations were not always unfounded, but her reactions were not welcomed by the two mothers. When Franco started school my father insisted that he should not sleep at Teresa's. At dusk, before Papà was due home, Angela would be sent to fetch Franco, an activity that she often turned into a licence to rough him up. This used to upset mamma Teresa:

'Giulia, I am sorry to have to say that she has done it again. She came and maltreated my little boy for nothing. He had not done anything wrong.'

Whether Franco was totally innocent or not, both mothers agreed that Angela was not the one to judge and to administer punishment. Mamma Giulia kept the misbehaviour by both Franco and Angela from our father.

Even if not much more experienced than her siblings, Angela was certainly more savvy and quick to understand the practicalities of life. When we were fussy and demanding, my mother used to tell us that unless we behaved she would leave us and go off to Lonthra, her Calabrian pronunciation for faraway London. On one occasion, I started crying and feeling miserable. Angela intervened:

'Stop it. Don't be daft. I am sure she has just gone to Zia Maria's for coffee and a chat and will soon come back.'

Following our breakfast, Mamma makes a last-minute check on our shoes, buttons, collars and the books and notebooks to be taken with us and then ... we are off to school. Mamma carries my satchel with books and a snack. It can be boiled or roasted chestnuts, or an apple or dried figs with walnuts. I like to be relieved of the burden of the heavy satchel but feel that Mamma looks awkward and ridiculous with it, like an oversized child.

When I grow up and have my own family I shall never carry my children's books.

But decades later I do just that, remembering my mother as well as wanting to help my son and, recently, my grandchildren.

When I started school in 1945 we lived in the Paracorio side of Delianuova in a house on a corner between the main avenue and a side street which rose steeply towards the hill. My parents rented the house from a tailor who reserved a room on the ground floor as his workshop. He was a young man nicknamed *u ballarinu* (the dancer) and I kept having this image of him dancing and pirouetting throughout the night in the streets of Delianuova – dancing on his own. I could not imagine that Deliese young women would indulge in such shameful pursuits. Though I enjoyed these dancing fantasies they did seem at odds with reality. The tailor was a quiet, serious and well-behaved man. I never learned his real name. Nicknames were frequent but what I did not know then was that they were often related to the activities of previous generations. It may have been his father or grandfather or an uncle who had been dancers.

We had an independent front door on the side street, the one where 'Ntoni used to stop with his goats. At the entrance a small door led to our toilet, no more than a deep hole in the ground, as proper sewerage was not yet available in Delianuova. This damp, low-ceiling room was at the back of the tailor's workshop and separated from it by a wall. A short flight of stairs from the front door led up to our kitchen at the back and our dining room at the front of the house. This was just on top of the workshop and had a pleasant balcony over the main street, Corso Umberto. The top floor had a good-sized bedroom at the front and two small ones at the back and side. At the back of the house, our kitchen opened into a small square shared by other houses. We had no garden. This was common in a town in which, for centuries, houses had been built next to each other for protection. Some families, like my Ietto grandparents, had small allotments where they grew vegetables.

Leaving our house we would walk along Corso Umberto towards Pedavoli where all the classrooms were located. This more middle-class side of the town was where most of the teachers lived. The corso evolved in a horseshoe pattern with the central part sitting on the slope and the two sides reaching down towards the valley. From Paracorio I struggled uphill towards Piazza Regina Elena where sits the parish Church of the Assumption.

On a spring morning the corso was full of life, with children emerging from houses and criss-crossing to meet their friends. Women greeting each other, some sweeping their threshold. Bed linen was shaken from windows. Balconies were full of pots of geraniums, basil, begonias and spider plants, their colours competing for attention with the colours of clothes hung up to dry. One very large house on the left - Palazzo Cordopatri - had neither plants nor washing. It was uninhabited and derelict. It changed ownership and was fully restored in the following decades. Next to it, a large side road ascended to i Lazzari where Teresa and her family lived. At the top of this steep road and in the midst of dereliction was a large house separated from the rest by a gate and front garden. It belonged to an old landowning family and the incumbent during my childhood was a much loved and respected doctor. An occasional glimpse up in that direction allowed me to see the first of the two secular, large pine trees that graced the town. Alas! it died in 2008, aged 300 years.

Just before the piazza on the right is a double fountain with spouts emerging from two carved heads attached to the wall. Next to it was - and still is - the grocery shop and house of my best friend Maria. We were in the same class. She would be waiting for us with her mother, Teresa, who would start talking to Mamma while I chatted with Maria. The two mothers were great friends and had married two friends. Giulia and Teresa grew up together and were united by the piazza - the playground of their own childhood. On the left-hand side, at the bottom of the ramp leading up to the church, was, in fact, my maternal grandfather's house with his café on the ground floor. On a sunny morning he would have a couple of tables outside it by the time we reached this part of the corso. He always waved at us, a friendly smile on his face.

Don Federico would soon position himself not far from Nonno's café. This aging, intelligent, small landowner, whose lands had by now gone, cultivated a passion for political commentaries: his own and other people's. With the end of fascism he was able to indulge openly in his passion. First thing in the morning he used to read the papers and then walk from his house across the piazza. He was ready to start talking about the latest news and comment on Don Sturzo or De Gasperi or the views of Indro Montanelli and on the reliability of the latest *di fondo* article – the editorial. As soon as he approached his corner a few men from all directions joined him to listen to his views and air their own. Meanwhile back home his wife – one of the best cooks in Delianuova – was preparing lunch for him and their large family. Their eldest daughter was managing a tobacco and grocery shop on the ground floor of their house. In less than two decades their youngest daughter – three years older than me – was to become one of my aunts.

Maria and I started walking while we chatted and giggled. We followed the corso to the right in its ascent towards my paternal grandparents' house. It was in Largo Rosario, a wide opening off the corso. The simple public fountain in its middle was accessible to thirsty or mischievous children. Opposite, on the other side of the corso were two large mansions belonging to different branches of the same landowning family. The Grecos were then resident and their houses well kept. One of the houses had an attractive corner balcony. Covered by a slanted little roof it was supported by a series of columns in the classical style. The other one, the larger of the two, had a lovely front garden full of palm trees. A double flight of stairs converged on the first floor of the house and its main entrance. The two houses were separated by a side road. The previous generation of owners joined them via a covered bridge on the first floor. I liked to look at this elegant construction that united families and yet I was never able to see anyone crossing it. I often thought that were I ever to become a resident of the smaller house I would spend most of my time on the little bridge looking at the people passing underneath and waving at my friends. I would also fill the corner balcony with flower pots and hang my washing from the balcony to give it some colour.

I kept wondering about the interior of these houses and at the people living in them. We occasionally saw the ladies at Sunday Mass. They had separate seating and kneeling furniture. I now know that the interior of the houses contained one of the best libraries of Calabria, recently sold to the small town of Scido and thus saved from the general decay of the houses. They have been uninhabited for many years. The family produced some very competent professionals including a doctor and – a few decades ago – a young, female mayor of Delianuova. Quite an achievement for a Calabrian woman to be one of the first female mayors in Italy.

A 1940s photographer took a shot of the stretch of the Paracorio corso in the opposite direction to which I was ascending to go to school. He placed himself just to the left of my favourite bridge uniting the two Greco mansions, thus, unfortunately, missing it. One of the two mansions is well visible on the right with its corner balcony. The enthusiasm for democratic governance after the decades of fascism led to unsightly graffiti. At the very end of the photo the pine tree is visible with, just in front of it, Nonno Nino's café and house. The Ristorante Albergo Aspromonte sounds grand, but I do not know of any Deliese who ever dined there. The Necchi sewing machines were beginning to sell well as women and men gradually became interested in new clothes after the war years. The shallow, large steps at the bottom left of the photo between the advertising signs for Albergo Aspromonte and Necchi lead up to Largo Rosario where the Ietto grandparents' house was.

We had reached the end of Paracorio. From now on it was a blissful descent across Pedavoli. One more dilapidated and deserted palazzo on the right. In this and in other large or small houses, the front doors were framed by green stone with small sculptures of monsters and flowers. They were not always clearly visible; the stone was often broken.

Maria and I reached our destination first. Angela would continue along the corso which now descended in its last section of the horseshoe. Her classroom was on a wide opening just past Piazza Delia. This piazza – now renamed Guglielmo Marconi – has civic connections. It was the site of the town hall built in the 1930s

3. A view of Paracorio in the 1940s

and it houses a town clock large and loud enough to be seen and heard from most places in Delianuova. Set on raised ground with two attractive flights of stairs leading down to the corso, Piazza Marconi is a large square where public seats shaded by holm oaks and fir trees give old people an opportunity to rest and chat with friends. The second large pine tree gracing Delianuova's landscape was planted in the nineteenth century near this section of the corso, on the other side of Piazza Guglielmo Marconi. The parish church for Pedavoli - the church of San Nicola - is in a valley off the main corso, way past the location of our old classrooms. An attractive crescent flight of stairs in *pietra verde* leads up to the church's three entrances.

A second postcard photo of the 1940s was taken from Piazza Delia. It has a panoramic view of Delianuova with the two secular pine trees at opposite sides of the horseshoe.

4. A view of Delianuova from Piazza Delia

Mamma Giulia's cooking: she keeps her promise

Pasta e ricotta: a gentle, summer dish

This is a dish Mamma prepared only occasionally, depending on the vagaries of 'Ntoni's delivery of ricotta cheese. It was always served as a lunch dish when Papà was away. He preferred stronger and more peppery meals.

You need fresh ricotta cheese, a very small amount of oil, some grated pecorino or parmigiano cheese, and pasta. Mamma always used smallish *conchigliette* – shells. They trap the ricotta cheese and thus enhance the flavour of the dish. The olive oil used by Mamma in all her recipes was always top quality. The freshness and quality of the ricotta is essential. I tried to make this dish with ricotta from British supermarkets and it is not nearly as good as it should be.

Cook your pasta in the usual way (see Chapter 5). While the pasta is boiling put some fresh ricotta into a shallow bowl adding a couple of spoonfuls of liquid from the cooking pasta. Lightly mash the ricotta with a fork. Drain the pasta, add it to the ricotta and mix together. Add a very small amount of oil and grated pecorino. Parmigiano will do if you cannot get pecorino.

2

Education, Education, Education

*All of us had a bit of schooling
In something and somehow:
hence education, God be praised,
is in our midst not hard to flaunt.*
Alexander Pushkin

Off to school we went. But there was no 'school' to go to. No single building could be identified as 'the school' until the late 1950s when one was built by my father and his brothers' firm as contractors for the local authority. During my five years of primary education and for a few more after, lessons were held in rooms rented here and there from private landlords.

My class was made up mainly of children of shopkeepers, well-to-do artisans and some less affluent professionals. Children from poor working-class or peasant families were enrolled but rarely attended, particularly in winter when they followed their mothers to the countryside for the olive harvest. The well-to-do landowners and professionals sent their children to private boarding schools in Reggio, Messina or, sometimes, further afield to Rome or Florence. Only the first five years of elementary education were available in Delianuova. Children whose parents were keen on academic education but could not afford boarding schools had to travel daily on rickety buses for quite some distance. Three further years of middle school later became available in Delianuova when the compulsory school age was raised in Italy from 11 to 14.

My classroom was in a dressmaker's house opposite Palazzo Soffrè. This early nineteenth-century building still retains some of its great architectural and stonemasonry works. My father considered it to be by far the best in Delianuova and one of the best in Calabria. A member of the family, the blind Felice, became a well-respected poet. He was often visited by his cousin, the composer Francesco Cilea, born in nearby Palmi. His works include *Adriana Lecouvrer* and *L'Arlesiana*. Local history records that in 1861, when Garibaldi was wounded in the Aspromonte battle, Domenico Soffrè provided assistance. He was the last mayor of Pedavoli, which was shortly to be merged with Paracorio to form the new town of Delianuova in 1878.

Close to the dressmaker's house was our teacher's home. This was convenient for her and had great advantages for us children. She occasionally disappeared to attend to her cooking or supervise her maid. We had a great time during her absences. One day the girls started playing at divining the future, at which one or two of the older ones declared themselves expert. I volunteered to have my fate disclosed. I dropped some ink on a piece of paper, then folded it and left it for a few seconds. Antonietta, the diviner, opened it. With a very serious expression on her face she looked at the shapes of the ink-blots for what seemed a very long time. She then foretold my future. It was as bleak as all her divinations. No white knight in armour on my life path.

Occasionally we would use our teacher's absences to pop into the nearby fields and relieve ourselves. It was a welcome break for me, as I hated the toilet facilities in the basement of the dressmaker's house. On a raised platform was a hole surrounded by rough concrete on which we sat. The roughness of the seat hurt my legs and the dirt left on it by previous users put me off the whole process.

When on our own in the classroom, we tried – often unsuccessfully – to control the noise. If it exceeded a certain level the dressmaker would reprimand us. We were in awe of her. She was called *a longa* – the long or tall one. In a town of people of low average height by Italian standards, she appeared very tall. I now suspect that this may have been the reason why she never married.

Macho Calabrian men may have taken her height as an affront to their masculinity.

On one occasion her imposing persona asserted itself towards a teacher rather than us. We often had supply teachers to take the place of our main schoolmistress. One such teacher was a timid, sweet, little woman. On this day she decided to keep us quiet by reading us stories from *Cuore* by Edmondo De Amicis. She was reading *Dagli Apennini alle Ande*, a story about a boy who leaves Italy for Argentina in search of his lost mother. She had left the family to work as a maid for a wealthy employer. The family had received no news for some time and the boy volunteered to go in search of her. Page after page of terrible suffering and anguish led to both teacher and her class sobbing and wailing uncontrollably. Suddenly the classroom door opened and *a longa* appeared, towering at the entrance:

'Unless you stop this nonsense and noise in my house I will eject you and your pupils from my premises and I will report you to the inspector.'

I never found out the end of the story until a few years ago when I decided to buy a copy of *Cuore* and read it myself.

Another supply teacher remains in my mind for different reasons. She was young and very pretty, with dark eyes and loose, wavy, black hair reaching to her shoulders. I kept receiving enquiries about her from my uncle Mimmo.

'How was your teacher dressed today? Did she mention where she might go after school? Did she say whether she is likely to spend some time in Delianuova or go away soon?'

I don't know whether these enquiries led to any interesting developments. He married someone else. But memories of this particular supply teacher were revived a few years ago. From the surname and family connections, I believe that she was a close relative – the mother or aunt – of the Italian secret-service agent Nicola Callipari. He was killed in the winter of 2005 by American forces in Iraq immediately after his successful negotiations to free the journalist Giuliana Sgrena, kidnapped by insurgents.

On sunny days this teacher took us to Piazza Delia. Its large, open spaces were often used for physical education sessions. We were made to march in military fashion. She taught us how to skip steps and re-align ourselves. I found these exercises very trying and could never march in step with the others – my left foot always got mixed up with the right.

Half-way through the morning we would have a picnic break. One spring two sisters, daughters of local landowners, joined the class temporarily in between moves from one boarding school to another. They usually sat apart and had no close friends in the class. Blonde – Assunta was sure that their hair had been dyed – and elegantly dressed, they stood out among us. One day, at the snack break they produced bread and chocolate cheese triangles. The eyes of some 20 children stared at the gold wrappings and chocolate filling, never seen by any of us before.

Chocolate and school bring back another unpleasant association. After the war the Americans sent packages of chocolate slabs to be distributed to schoolchildren. One day our teacher told us that the chocolate pieces would be distributed the next day.

'Dear children, you are very lucky to receive all this chocolate from the Americans. If you want, you can leave a little bit of your portion for my little boy.'

The next day she distributed our rations and we left a small piece for her child. All of us but for one girl, Rosaria. She was the daughter of a strong-minded, strong-willed carpenter who had fathered ten children. In a quivering, low voice she said:

'My father told me not to leave any of my chocolate behind but to take it all home.'

I felt sorry for her. I became troubled, unable to decide whether her father was right or not.

Over a year earlier Angela had been singled out for special generosity by the American soldiers. By the end of 1943 the Allied forces had secured control from the fascist troops over Sicily and started advancing north. As the story was related later by my mother and other relatives, a small contingent of American soldiers passed through Delianuova. They were welcomed and cheered by the Deliese women, children and old people. Angela had managed to sneak out to the very front of the small crowd in Largo Rosario where my grandparents' house was located. She cheered with particular enthusiasm, jumping up and down and shouting 'Evviva, evviva i mericani!' (Hurrah, hurrah for Americans!). The soldiers responded with laughs and ... sweets. One of them managed to find in Delianuova old relatives of his father who had emigrated to America. They communicated reasonably well, as he had learned some Calabrian dialect from his parents. These were the only soldiers ever seen in Delianuova during the war. Battles and bombing were, mercifully, kept away from my little town.

On one occasion, and to my great amazement, I became a sort of teacher. Onna Peppina a Bagnarota vecchia – Signora Peppina, the old woman from Bagnara – came to Delianuova once or twice a week to bring fish from the Tyrrhenian coastal town of Bagnara. Quite a few Bagnarote used to come to Delianuova with their wares. Onna Peppina was the oldest and seemed in charge of the younger women. Their men would fish during the night and the women take their loads after dawn to have it in the markets of various small towns later the same morning. They made the journey of several kilometres, mostly uphill, carrying on their heads large, shallow baskets full of anchovies or sardines. They walked fast and yet very elegantly, as their loads forced them to keep their heads erect and their bodies well balanced. Sometimes they got lifts from passing carts or, more rarely, lorries for part of their journey. They dressed in old-fashioned costumes, with a shirt tucked into a number of pleated skirts that reached to their ankles, revealing only their dark, hard-skinned, bare feet. Now and then they brought pots and pans or crockery to be bartered for dry beans or oil or chestnuts.

Onna Peppina was feared by most children for her fierce demeanour and sharp tongue. Occasionally she would become violent. This was usually in response to the provocation of children who would shout insults or even throw stones at her. She was friendly with my mother, who always bought her wares. On this day, during one of those blissful periods when our teacher was attending to more important affairs at home, Onna Peppina appeared at the classroom door instilling immediate silence and fear. She looked around and then signalled to me to approach her. Terror gripped me as I slowly moved towards her. When I reached her she smiled and asked me to bring my pencil and sit down with her on the staircase outside the classroom. She produced a piece of white paper and, timidly and gently, asked me to teach her how to write her full name. I was stunned and speechless.

Most of our first year at school was spent doing page after page of muscle-control writing. We started with *aste*, little vertical strokes repeated thousands of times until we learned to do them straight and evenly spaced. We then moved to writing vowels, each one for weeks on end till we managed to do them in a way that satisfied our teacher. I still blame my poor handwriting as an adult on the painful memories of those forced repetitions.

In later years we were introduced to more interesting activities: some reading, copying passages from our textbook, dictation, arithmetic, poetry. Our main teacher used to receive a magazine for primary-school teachers sent by the Ministry of Education. When the magazine arrived with its thin, light blue paper, she opened it and talked to us about its contents. She then set us some work from it: an arithmetic problem or dictation of a poem.

Learning poems by heart was a type of homework I found very tedious. I kept reading, rereading and repeating the lines throughout the afternoon. But, as evening approached, I became more and more muddled and worried about my performance the next day. I wished for a world free of rote learning.

How wonderful if we children could remain toddlers forever. We would be free to move about and enjoy ourselves; have lots of attention and cuddles from our parents and ... no duty to memorize poems!

Dictation, with or without punctuation, was a common classroom activity. In general, dictation is not so difficult for Italian children because the language is phonetic. However, our daily language was not Italian but the Calabrian dialect. So our class had to get used to words rarely used at home and in our everyday life. One year our final exam required a test of dictation without punctuation. We had to insert the right punctuation in the passage while the teacher was reading with the appropriate pauses. We were worried. This appeared to be a most difficult task. How were we to know whether a word should be followed by full stop or semicolon or colon? The test took place in the presence of an inspector. He sat at the teacher's desk while she, standing in front of it and facing her pupils, read the chosen passage. She wanted her class to do well and, in preparation for this big day, she told us:

'So children, remember to look carefully at my face while I read to you: one wink means a comma; if both eyes wink use a semicolon; when I press my lips you must use a full stop.'

On the day things did not go to plan. The sight of her funny faces had the whole class in uncontrollable laughter.

I still look back at this episode of school life with a mixture of disapproval and amusement. It seems that similar tricks are being introduced into British schools. In October 2002 a *Guardian* article reported a variety of expedients being used to improve the exam performance of schoolchildren. Among the 26 tricks used, the very first one reads: 'Silently indicating to children if they have got a question wrong by grimacing or shaking head, and conversely indicating correct answer by means of nodding.'

At times we were asked to do summaries of passages we read in our textbook. One day our teacher set us the task of reading a story about foxes and then writing a summary of it in our notebooks. She then left us to it. While she was away, a discussion started among us as to what a summary is and how it should be done. Assunta had the answer:

'Writing a summary is very easy. A summary must be shorter than the full passage. So all we have to do is copy out only some of the lines. I will copy one every three lines.'

'What do I do when a word is split between two lines?' asks Carmela.

'Well, you copy only half the word!'

Many children took Assunta's advice. She was a couple of years older than most of us and commanded respect.

Mamma Giulia's cooking: fish on the Aspromonte hills

Acciughe fritte

Anchovies were the most common fish on our table in the post-World War II years. The Bagnarote women brought them to us now and then. The sea around Scylla did produce luxury fish such as the swordfish for which the area is renowned. I suspect that the best fish made its way to upmarket restaurants in Reggio or Messina or to the tables of rich landowners. Mamma made the best out of anchovies and they were delicious.

Most women in Delianuova, including my mother, would cook them whole because their men enjoyed heads, entrails and all. I love them but I prefer to remove the heads and, trailing behind them, the entrails. When I manage to get them from my London or Rome fishmonger I hold each anchovy with my left hand and pull off the head and entrails with my right hand. I then wash the headless anchovies and pat them dry with kitchen paper.

They can be fried plain or coated with flour. When removing them from the frying pan place on a shallow dish which you will have covered with a couple of layers of kitchen paper to absorb the extra fat. Pat them on top with extra paper.

Acciughe fritte make a lovely canapé with your aperitif as well as a main course.

Acciughe al forno

Lay the anchovies on a shallow oven dish and sprinkle with bread-crumbs, finely chopped up garlic and tiny bits of pre-peeled, succulent, fresh tomatoes. Cover with foil and bake for about 20 minutes at 200 degrees. Remove the foil for the last five minutes.

In London, I have used this recipe for sprats. Being bigger than anchovies they need an extra five minutes in the oven. The sprats are slightly sweeter than the anchovies and I find that they are better without the addition of tomato pieces.

Tortino di acciughe e patate

During a recent visit to Rome my sister cooked for me this delicious dish. Use some 400gm of fresh anchovies. Clean and dry them as above. Peel two or three large potatoes and slice them thin. Spread a small amount of oil in an oven-proof dish and then place in it a layer of potatoes followed by a layer of anchovies. Spread on top some small flakes of peeled tomatoes followed by another layer of potatoes and more tomato flakes. Cover loosely with tin foil and bake for some 30 minutes at 200 degrees. Remove the foil for the last five minutes.

Nannata

This is a dish that is no longer available and rightly so. When I was a child I could not understand the meaning of *nannata*. I only knew that it referred to very small fish whose tiny eyes disturbed me even more than the eyes of bigger ones. *Nannata* is the Calabrian word for *neo-nata* or newly born. These tiny creatures often came lumped up in small masses that the women tried to separate before frying. Mamma never liked to cook them. She only bought them when nothing else was available. I am delighted to report that fishing *nannata* is now illegal.

Stoccafissu/Baccalà

This was a common dish in Calabria where dried cod was widely available. For centuries it reached the Mediterranean countries from the Nordic regions. Mamma soaked it in cold water for a whole day, changing the water from time to time. When fully reconstituted she cut it in single-portion chunks and pat dried them. The fish was then lightly covered in flour and fried at high temperature for a couple of minutes on each side. Ready on the side were a chopped onion and some chopped tomatoes, those preserved during the summer. You can use tinned tomatoes. She fried the onion very slightly, adding the chopped tomatoes and then the fish. At this point the temperature should be lowered to allow the fish to cook through for about 20 minutes. Half-way through the cooking, she would add some plain, pitted black olives, a vegetable never in short supply in Calabrian homes.

3

Improving minds, skills and souls

It wasn't the awareness of how beautiful it was
that meant so much to us,
or of how good the atmosphere was, but the feeling of community,
the way we all felt a kinship with the objects and events of our
existence.
Erich Maria Remarque

My teachers must take some credit for educating me in the arts of multiplication, division, reading and writing, if not punctuation. However, the mystery of how some of us acquired a few academic skills lies not so much in what we did at school as in what we did after school. My parents insisted that we should go to after-school private tuition classes.

Throughout their lives my parents regretted the lack of opportunities to continue their studies when young. They had only primary education and both felt very strongly the lack of further academic advancement. My mother used to tell us that in her school days she had won a prize for her ability to conjugate the verbs *essere* (to be) and *avere* (to have) in front of a visiting inspector. But she always added that all this had been useless, as she never learned anything else. Both my parents felt shy, embarrassed and at a disadvantage when dealing with educated people. They were at their strongest when talking about building works (my father) and cooking (my mother). These were the occasions when their faces lit up in front of educated strangers. They encouraged us to continue our studies both explicitly and just by being supportive of our efforts. My mother succeeded in her plans to send me to after-school and vacation classes in Delianuova. My sister and brother were also enrolled, though they often found more pleasant ways of spending their afternoons.

All three of us would start from home together and usually by ourselves. Delianuova children went about freely. There was no fear of possible danger. Most people knew each other and their children, and would readily help a child if necessary. Cars, motorcycles and even bicycles were rare. The only motor vehicle we saw daily was the postal bus, the *corriera* to and from Gioia Tauro. This service was also available when the British traveller and writer Norman Douglas visited the area in 1911 and 1937. He did not avail himself of it. He preferred to walk from Gioia to Delianuova. Walking was his preferred method of moving around Calabria because, 'Cars don't help you to know people.' In a similar vein, he also declined letters of introduction to local dignitaries and gentry, as was the accepted practice for travellers, preferring to get his information from the more common people and his rest and food in whatever facilities the place could offer. Like Gissing and Lear before him he discovered that these were often pretty basic in Calabria.

On the way to our destination, Angela and Franco might meet a friend. More interesting plans for the afternoon developed and off they would go. They might join me later or not. Sometimes Angela came with me and then sneaked out, particularly at the start of embroidery, an activity she hated.

The sessions were run by three genteel women fallen on hard times: a widow and her two young daughters, Filumena (called Filuzza) and Checchina, one of the many nicknames for Francesca. They came from a different town where their house had burned down because of an electrical fault. The widow refused to have electricity in all her subsequent homes. Checchina was the youngest. She was at the time studying in a different town to become a primary-school teacher. She used to spend her winters there and school holidays in Delianuova where she helped to improve the family finances. Filuzza was known as one of the best embroiderers in town and this is what she taught us girls. She was very kind but known to suffer from 'attacks of nerves'. We joined these three welcoming women and sat on their floor or on small stools in their main room.

I was particularly pleased when Checchina was around. Beautiful, with long, black, lustrous hair, she was very gentle though firm. She paid particular attention to me and my best friend Maria, and taught us basic academic skills. Maria was a tiny girl like me. She had a happy nature and twinkling eyes. We were very fond of each other and shared everything including handkerchiefs. We often blew our noses in each other's snot. My eagerness to go to these afternoon sessions was partly due to the prospect of continuing the chatter Maria and I had started in the morning at school. Checchina gave extra arithmetic work to Maria:

'Maria, you must learn to multiply, add and divide very quickly. You may have a shop to run in the future. Grazietta, meanwhile, you read this story.'

Maria did indeed take over the family grocery business later in life and developed it very effectively. This did not prevent her from raising a family of five.

When Checchina was away attending to her studies Maria and I devoted extra time to embroidery. Filuzza taught us various stitches and told us about patterns and colours. She guided us but left us to choose.

'I think I will do my ducks yellow and the grass blue. What will you do Maria?'

'Oh! I like red. I will have red ducks and green grass.'

We talked and talked about our choices. Embroidery work was fun at both the planning and execution stages. It was also satisfying for me to have a finished piece of work to show my parents and relatives. They all praised me and sometimes gave me a little reward money. But on one occasion I became upset when my uncle Angelo started teasing me. He snatched my embroidered piece and threatened to wipe his nose with it.

'Stop it, you stupid boy. Give it back to me! Go away and leave me with Grazietta and her beautiful work,' rebuffed my grandmother.

Filuzza was very interested in the town's goings-on. She would often try to get information from us about our families and relations. She seemed particularly interested to find out the whereabouts, activities and interests of my paternal uncles. Her younger and more beautiful sister became engaged very early on. One summer her fiancé appeared on leave from his military service. He sat in a corner and looked at Checchina while she taught us. He kept making teasing remarks and puns about the word 'exercise', which she used for our work while he used it for his military training. She seemed embarrassed and uneasy. The widow moved her chair to gain more visibility of the two lovers. She was looking out for signs of impropriety and displays of affection. We hoped to see some such signs. But alas! we were disappointed over and over again.

The widow was stern and formidable, yet very caring of us children. She looked after our souls and made sure that we started each session with a prayer. We were made to recite another one midway through the session and to end with one of thanks. She stood facing us underneath a picture of Jesus, the Sacred Heart. Day after day I would look at that picture:

I wish I also had my heart on the outside. Then the doctors could see what is wrong with it and fix it.

Back home it was time for *merenda*, the late afternoon snack, a piece of bread with oil sometimes sprinkled with sugar (yes, sugar!) or spread with *trema trema* - wobble wobble - the jelly made from pork fat. We snatched it from Mamma's hands and rushed out to play in the street where our friends were already enjoying themselves. Occasionally Mamma signalled to me to stay behind and I knew that she had a treat for my *merenda* - *uovo sbattuto*. She would hand me a bowl with an egg yolk and plenty of sugar and I would beat the mixture into a smooth cream, the basis for *zabaione*. I enjoyed the process. The texture changes from granular to smooth; the colour from intense to soft, delicate yellow. Even more, I enjoyed eating the final product. Angela and Franco resented this special treatment and would often appear and dip their fingers into the mixture to partake of my treat. While we played outside, Mamma often sat at her dining room balcony and did little, quiet jobs.

Today she *spuntica* – snaps the heads off and removes strings from – runner beans. She keeps and eye on us and on the passers-by in the corso. The standard greetings follow. One that intrigues me in my childhood and still amuses me many decades later is:

Passer-by: 'What are you doing?'

Sitting woman or old man: '*Accà*' (As you see).

I keep wondering when I would be old enough to go around asking women what they are doing sitting outside their front doors or at their balconies.

As darkness falls Mamma calls us in: dinner is ready and Papà is back. We start with *zuppa di fagioli freschi e pasta* followed by home-made salami or salted cheese. Bread and olives are always on the table and so are wine and water. A piece of fruit ends our meal. In the war year the meals were more frugal and what appeared on the table was largely a matter of chance. I remember lots of butter bean soups, boiled or roasted chestnuts, apples and mandarins.

Mamma Giulia's cooking: nourishing summer soups

Runner beans with pasta

You need fresh runner beans, oil, garlic, tomatoes and small pasta shapes which could be spaghetti/linguine cut into small pieces.

Top the beans, remove any side strings and cut them into 1-2cm-long pieces. In a saucepan lightly fry 2-3 garlic cloves and add some peeled, fresh or tinned tomatoes cut in small pieces. After three to four minutes add your beans. Stew for some 10-15 minutes according to how tough the beans are. Separately boil the pasta; do not cook fully but leave it quite hard – some two minutes before full cooking time. When ready, pour some liquid from the pasta into a bowl and keep aside. Add the pasta with a small amount of liquid to the vegetable stew. Let the beans and pasta finish the cooking together. You can add more cooking water from your bowl. Add more olive oil before serving.

If you have some left over, this dish is delicious the next day. I always make sure to cook enough for a second meal. Store in your fridge both the leftover soup and the extra pasta cooking water. The next day heat up the soup adding some of the pasta water (pre-heated). You may also add a little extra oil.

Pasta e cavolfiore

The above process can also be used with cauliflower – Mamma liked the white variety. This dish is particularly delicious with Romano cauliflower, of the brilliant green and inverted cone shape. Cut the cauliflower into small florets and then proceed as for the dish above. Again this thick soup is very good the next day.

Pasta e broccoli: two versions

The two dishes above are thick soups often served in Calabria as healthy family fillers. Good fillers of pasta with a variety of vegetables can be had as a *pasta asciutta*. In Italian *asciutta* means dry. Of course, no cooked pasta is literally dry. The term *pasta asciutta* is used to designate a pasta dish which is not broth-based, the type of dish you eat with a fork rather than a spoon. In the following chapters I will give several other *pasta asciutta* dishes. Here I want to present a type which both my husband and I particularly like: *pasta e broccoli*. I have two versions for the broccoli, both to be used as dressing for pasta. I use *conchiglie* or *penne* or other short pasta for both versions of the dish.

In the first version I lightly fry some chopped garlic, add the dark, green broccoli florets and let them simmer, adding small amounts of water now and then. I like to use the boiling water from the cooking pasta. When the pasta is almost cooked and drained I add it to the broccoli and stir. Sprinkle with black pepper and serve hot.

The second version is one used in other parts of Italy. You need some five anchovy fillets for 150gm of pasta. The broccoli florets are first boiled in plenty of water. Half-way through the cooking process, drain them but retain their cooking water. Put the anchovy fillets cut in small pieces in a large frying pan. Add a couple of spoonfuls of water from the boiled florets. Stir and mash the anchovies to make them into a semi-liquid paste. Add the drained florets and stir while they cook together for a couple of minutes. Meanwhile cook your pasta in the saved broccoli water with some addition if necessary. When almost ready, drain it and add the pasta to the frying pan with the florets and anchovy paste. Let the mixture cook for a couple of minutes, occasionally adding some water if it becomes too dry. Serve hot.

In both versions of pasta and broccoli I add a little fresh olive oil before serving.

4

Affairs of the heart:
number one

heart: n. 1. the hollow muscular organ in vertebrates whose contractions propel the blood through the circulatory system.

Collins English Dictionary

I knew that my heart was different. My mother talked about it to friends and relatives. Angela, Franco and I had often touched each other's breast to feel the noise. My heart won the competition as regards noise level. Nobody seemed to know what was wrong. Mamma would take me to any doctor passing by for a couple of days or spending his holidays in the cool of the Delianuova hills. They put their ears on my chest and pronounced that it was bad but they could not tell what was wrong or what to do about it. The last one told my mother:

'She is not going to make it past *lo sviluppo*. You have two other children; be content with those.'

Lo sviluppo – 'the development' – was a euphemism for menstruation. These words by the Aesculapian savant stayed with me for a long time. My menstruation was always extremely painful till the birth of my son in 1975.

There were advantages to be had from my noisy heart. My parents and relatives were always gentle and extra caring about me. My mother secured the best food she could get for me, including my beloved *zabaione*. There were other signs of gentle concern. My paternal grandfather, before his training as a builder, had a short

31

period as an apprentice to a cobbler. He never practised, but what he learned turned out to be useful in later life. He saved shoe-repair money for his family of nine and continued shoe-mending for us, his first grandchildren. He was always keen to add hobnails to the soles of our shoes to make them last longer and got thin ones for me to avoid burdening my shoes with too much extra weight.

My mother's concern was not without its problems. After the war many friends and relatives who had emigrated sent packages, largely of clothes. One such person, Arcangela *a musca* (the fly), was often praised by my parents for being a very loyal and helpful friend. On one occasion she included in her package to us from Cleveland, Ohio, 'a new medicine which cures everything'. This was penicillin, sent in a set of small double phials, one of white powder and one of liquid. Mamma seized the chance to cure her little daughter with this wonder drug. I was injected with the painful mixture every six hours, night and day, for a week.

From a corner of her bedroom I watch her operations with anxiety. She prepares her syringe. Pierces one phial. Extracts the liquid from it. Injects it into the phial with the powder. Shakes the mixture. Extracts the new liquid from the phial. It is now in her syringe. I follow it and its hated needle. I tighten my quivering lips. I do not want to cry. She urges me to be brave. I take down my knickers. I lie down on her bed. I grip the bed cover with my hands. The pain caused by the needle is short and sharp. The pain caused by the liquid lasts longer. Eventually it all passes. As soon as the pain subsides I feel a sense of relief. I will be able to relax for a few hours. An hour or two before the next injection, fear grips me again.

My mother's other concern was the summer picnics to our nearest mountain plateau: I Piani di Carmelia. During the summer, many families went there now and then for daily excursions; others stayed longer, living in wooden huts. It was always talked of as a wonderful place. Children loved the picnics and looked forward to them for months in advance. The hard ascent was graced by acacias, oleanders, broom and spider orchid as well as chestnuts, beaches and firs.

Norman Douglas passed through I Piani on his climb from Delianuova to Montalto and up to the highest point in Aspromonte.
There he saw the statue of the Redeemer looking towards Reggio. It
was originally dragged up in pieces from Delianuova. Having made
it on foot from Gioia Tauro on the Tyrrhenian coast to Delianuova,
Douglas did not linger in my little town: all he wanted was a guide
to take him to Bova on the Ionian coast. It is only a few kilometres
as the crow flies but a very hard endeavour when roads and paths
were almost non-existent. Reading Douglas brings back memories
of adults' conversations about towns and people on the Ionian
coast. When referring to Bovalino or Africo or Bova, the Deliesi
often made a grimace with their mouth and an outward gesture
with their hand to signify places almost impossible to reach. In fact
the Aspromonte massif, now declared a national park, has, through
the past centuries, separated the Tyrrhenian communities from
the Ionian ones. It made interaction between them very difficult.
'Aspromonte deserves its name,' wrote Douglas of this harsh, windy
and cold mountain. But he was too keen to discover more and
more of his beloved Calabria to be deterred. He was directed to a
local boss who knew the town and its people and who commanded
their respect. But alas! He was by then an old man more interested
in playing with his little grandson than in further exploring the
Aspromonte. He warned of the dangers of trying to cross the massif.
'To Montalto, yes; to Bova, no.' A younger guide was found. They
went through chestnuts and beeches and 'magnificent groves of fir',
then 'odorous pines interspersed with Mediterranean heath'.

Mamma always insisted that I should not go on these excursions to I Piani di Carmelia but stay behind with her. She would
coax me by taking me for little walks nearby or preparing a special
meal for the two of us, such as *pasta e ricotta*. But it was not much
of a consolation. I knew that, on their return, Angela, Franco and
our friends would talk endlessly about how much they had enjoyed
themselves. I resented my mother. I thought that she did not want
to go and that she sacrificed me to keep her company. Only much
later did I realize that, of course, the opposite was true. She must
have thought that I could not make the long steep walks on uneven
paths and decided to stay behind with me.

I was also excluded from seaside holidays. My aunt Maria, my mother's older sister, suffered from bone problems which gradually reduced her mobility. It had been suggested that she should spend a fortnight a year by the seaside, burying her legs in the hot sand. She used to go to Bagnara with her numerous children and take my sister. On her return Angela went on and on about how wonderful it was to be at the seaside, how huge the sea was and what fun she had had with the other children.

I long to look at the sea. I have heard that it consists of an enormous amount of water and I imagine it like a huge rectangular tub. Eventually, at the age of eight, I am taken on a day trip to Reggio. We pass through olive, orange and mandarin groves as well as vineyards. As we approach Scilla I glimpse the immense, blue expanse of water. The earlier sickness and vomit caused by the winding hillside roads are soon forgotten when I am in Reggio's Via Marina next to the sea. I feel totally overwhelmed by it: the colours, the noise, the movement, the foam as the waves break near us. I can hardly believe my eyes.

'Where does it end?'

'It continues forever. It does not end.'

I feel uneasy. After a minute or two my speech returns:

'How can there be nothing at the other end? Look, there seem to be buildings over there far away. What is it?'

'It is Messina.'

I have heard of Messina. I feel more reassured. It is not never ending after all. Soon, too soon, they tear me away for shopping. The men have already left us to attend to business. We walk uphill towards the cathedral and Via Garibaldi. I feel stunned at the sight of the many trees lining these sights. Their foliage is shaped into cubes!

'Can trees grow like this?'

'No, No, Grazietta. They are trimmed into these shapes.'

'Why? They look strange. I prefer the shape of our trees. The leaves grow where they like.'

There starts my lifelong dislike of topiaries. Time for lunch and reunion with the men. My first experience of a meal in a restaurant. We sit around a table and a lady comes and greets us warmly; she knows the adults. I observe the other customers, the waiter, the people walking outside. I expect the food to be picked up from the kitchen and brought to us by Zia Velia or Mamma. When a waiter brings it and serves us I feel a sense of unease.

Angela used to boast to her friends that her little sister had a funny heart. She and I occasionally allowed other children to feel the noise in my chest. One day a girl dared to ask me, in front of my sister, whether I would soon die of it. But it is one thing to boast about your little sister's physical peculiarities and another to accept something as preposterous as her death. The girl received from Angela such a wallop in words and deeds that nobody ever dared to pop that silly question again. Not in front of her. As for me, I usually replied:

'I am not going to die yet. When I am old, maybe 25 or 30, then I will die.'

I had longer-term plans for my life. I wanted to get married and have children. I had set my sight on two nice, well-behaved little boys as potential husbands. Listening to adults' conversations, I had heard often enough that mothers of marriageable young men do not want weak, sickly women as brides for their sons. I was determined to gain a reputation for strength and health. Every time I was playing in the streets and one of the targeted boys' mothers passed by, I would start skipping with whatever rope was available. Thinking back, it is very unlikely that anyone ever noticed my modest skipping skills. If the targeted mothers did see me, the breathlessness caused by my exertions must certainly have convinced them that I was unfit to be a future bride for their darling sons.

Mamma Giulia's cooking: egg dishes

Egg *zabaione* was a treat designed to strengthen our bodies. I had it frequently. The other members of the family had it when ill or convalescing. The whole family had eggs cooked in a variety of ways on a regular basis.

Uova al pomodoro: eggs fried in tomatoes

On a summer day, when in Italy, I use San Marzano tomatoes. Mamma used to dip them in boiling water, drain them, peel and cut them into small pieces. When in Delianuova in winter she used the San Marzano tomatoes prepared during the summer and preserved in bottles. In London I now use chopped tomatoes from tins, adding bits of fresh, very ripe tomatoes. For two to three eggs I use about 200gm of tinned tomatoes.

The tomatoes – whether fresh or tinned – should be put in a frying pan with a small amount of oil. Let them cook gently for a few minutes, stirring from time to time. Add the eggs and let them cook slowly. Gently move the tomatoes away from the egg white to allow it to cook through. After three or four minutes use a spatula to carefully turn over the egg. Occasionally I put a British touch to this dish by adding bacon cut into small pieces into the frying pan. I first cut off most of the bacon fat and I always do the frying in olive oil rather than butter.

Frittata di zucchine e fiori

Omelettes are a staple of most cuisines, particularly the poor ones, and the Calabrian is no exception. Mamma often made them with courgettes and/or their flowers.

'Grazia, always choose your courgettes firm and thin. Those you get in London are too big.'

Slice your courgette first vertically in a cross and then horizontally into thin quasi-triangular shapes. Fry them lightly and then remove the excess oil or, better still, use a clean frying pan in which you put the fried courgettes without the oil. Raise the temperature and pour over the beaten eggs. Turn over twice.

In Italy the courgettes used to be sold with their flowers attached. More recently, flowers can be bought separately from courgettes. Sometimes Mamma used both flowers and courgettes in her omelettes. She would remove the stamens and the spiky green sepals from the flowers before cutting them into small bits ready for the omelette.

Leftover omelettes

A variety of leftovers can be used to make tasty omelettes: from broccoli to cauliflower to potatoes to spinach to spaghetti/linguine. Chop up the vegetables finely and lightly fry them before adding the beaten eggs. When you use potatoes, you can add a chopped onion and fry it together with the potatoes. The extra fat should be removed before pouring the beaten egg in. I often use leftover potatoes such as roasted ones.

Excellent omelettes can also be made with leftover spaghetti/linguine, particularly those dressed with tomato sauce. I often cook a little extra of this pasta to make sure I have some left over for a next-day omelette. Some 20gm is enough for a two-egg omelette. Cut up the spaghetti and place it in your frying pan with the addition of a little oil. Stir it and spread it out over the pan. Add the beaten egg and proceed.

When I have no other fresh vegetable or leftover, I use chopped parsley. I mix it up with the beaten egg rather than fry separately as I would do with other vegetables.

Mamma's omelettes always came out a perfect shape: well cooked but still soft on the inside. Her example was a hard one to follow. But I tried. At first, one or two fell from my plate as I tried to turn them over. I learned with time. The shape has never been as perfect as hers. But does it matter? The taste is good.

5

Affairs of the heart: number two

'Friend of my heart, you are not well.'
'Leave me. I am in love.'
Alexander Pushkin

Yes, I was keen to marry and have cute little children. I knew that giving birth involved pain. All due to the opening of the belly button out of which emerges the baby. Marriage, sex and children were closely linked in my mind. I had this idea of a one-to-one correspondence between an individual sex act, whatever that was, and conception.

It was not till later when I was around 12 or 13 during our summer holidays from Rome that one of my youngest aunts took me into her confidence. She was in her early 20s, and her eyes were set on a young man. But rumour had it that he was a womanizer and had an intimate relationship with a girl who was therefore 'ruined' and whose family might have insisted on marriage. I asked when the baby was due and auntie said that, as far as she knew, there was no baby on the way. I thus learned that sex does not always lead to conception.

On one rare occasion when my parents were both away, my sister and I were looked after by Caterina, a friend's daughter who was older than us. Franco was at Mamma Teresa's. All three of us girls slept in the big bed. They thought I was asleep and I pretended to be because I realized that their whispering could lead to interesting discoveries. Angela asked questions about what men and women did in bed. Caterina mentioned two intriguing things. Men massage the breasts of women. Men have white liquid coming out of their penises. I fell asleep at the crucial moment. It took many more years to discover how such a liquid is produced, where it ends up and by what process.

As regards the massaging of breasts I was convinced of its connection to the production of milk for the future baby. I imagined that, for the duration of the pregnancy, there was this nightly tedious job that parents were prepared to perform to produce food for their, yet unborn, baby. My aunt Velia was pregnant. Both she and my uncle looked tired to me – no doubt the effect of sleepless exertions to produce milk for my future cousin.

My friend Maria and I knew that the midwife delivered babies and was the first to see the newborn and to pronounce whether it was a boy or a girl.

'Grazia, how does she know if it is a boy or a girl? The baby is not yet dressed in boys' or girls' clothes, and it doesn't have fully grown hair. So how does the midwife know?'

'Maria, might the midwife look to see if there is a willie?'

'Oh, no! She would not do such a shocking thing!'

Sex and love were never discussed in front of the children. But there was plenty of chatter, particularly among women, about who misbehaved with whom or who was in love with whom. My mother gossiped with friends and relations. She always urged silence whenever my sister approached.

'Grazietta is *carta bianca* (a white, unstained piece of paper) on the facts of life. She would not understand. You can talk in front of her but, for God's sake, not in front of Angela.'

They underestimated my ability to understand and to deceive them. Marriage and love were in everybody's mind and not just mine. Love of the premarital kind was supposed to be confined to longing looks at a distance. Betrothed couples could see each other when the fiancé visited his beloved, but only under the watchful eye of a chaperon, usually the girl's mother. Opportunities for young men and women to meet face to face or be in the same room were very rare. Wedding parties were such welcome occasions, though the parents and older relatives were never away from the dance rooms.

But young people found their ways. Every now and then it was rumoured that a girl had 'run away'. She had eloped with a young man. I felt sorry for them.

Did they take comfortable shoes? Are they running out of breath? Can they stop to catch their breath?

The elopement was often due to family opposition to the union because the position of one of the partners was considered unsuitable. Sometimes the two families connived to avoid the expense of wedding parties.

Cupid was, at times, encouraged by the use of *sensali*. These specialist intermediaries were entrusted by the parents to scan the town and its neighbourhoods for suitable marriage partners for their sons or daughters. The main advantage of using intermediaries was their ability to match social positions. They often became involved in discussions about the dowry of the potential bride. *Sensali* were also involved in matches between men who had emigrated to Australia, the USA or South America, and chaste, hard-working, God-fearing girls from Calabria.

One of my older cousins, whose family could not provide a dowry, married a well-off man she had never met before. He was known to her parents from before his emigration as a caring, honest and sensible man. The wedding ceremony was performed separately in the two continents and the consent given by proxy. When she joined him in Australia it was as his wife.

How can she bear to be married to a man she does not know? And to go so far away from her family?

The separation of couples and families was very common. During the war years my father and some of my uncles were away for long periods. As I grew older they were all back. But I knew that, in most families, men had to go away looking for work. Keeping in touch was very difficult when you could not read or write and the letters took such a long time to arrive. My aunt Maria, who had benefited from five years of compulsory education, often wrote and read letters for women whose menfolk were away. One day I was at her house while she discussed with a woman what should be put in the letter to her husband. Following some practical details about health, the children, the parents and the pig, Zia Maria asked what she wanted her to put at the end:

'Your most affectionate wife or your loving wife? Hugs or kisses?'

They both blushed and so did I. The woman laughed coyly:

'Oh, I do not know about such things. You know better. Write what you think is appropriate. But remember, somebody else will read the letter to my husband when it reaches him.'

I don't know how my sensible and sensitive aunt resolved the problem. I suspect that many men in Australia and other countries in various continents received from their wives the same written expressions of wifely affection.

Mamma Giulia's cooking: the basics of southern Italian cuisine

Salsa di pomodoro

The simple *salsa di pomodoro* is the mainstay of Italian and particularly southern Italian cooking. It is not specifically a Calabrian dish but I give it here because it is used in some of the Calabrian dishes given elsewhere in the book. The main ingredient for the *salsa*, the tomato, is not an indigenous product. As the historian John Dickie reminds us, the *pomo d'oro* - golden apple - came to southern Italy via the Spanish rulers, having reached Spain from her colonies in South America where it originated.

British families have their own little ways of making gravy: some use fresh water, some use water from boiled potatoes and some use stock cubes. Similarly, every Italian region and almost every family has its own little secret on how to produce the best tomato sauce. Here I give Mamma's version. The real secret is in the quality and freshness of the ingredients, in this case the tomatoes and olive oil.

For tomato sauce you need *passata* which is the extracted juice and pulp from tomatoes, leaving out skins and seeds. There is an essential tool in Italian cooking designed to separate the peel and seeds from the pulp: the moulinette, which can now be bought in most British department stores.

Passata is best made from fresh tomatoes of which the top

quality are the San Marzano ones: long, deep-red tomatoes from the Campania region but available throughout Italy to use fresh in sauces or for preservation in tins and bottles. To prepare passata from fresh ingredients wash the tomatoes, open out in half and pass through the moulinette. Alternatively you can cut the tomatoes in half, boil them on their own for 5-10 minutes and then put them through the moulinette. If fresh tomatoes of a good ripe variety are not available for first-class passata – and they are not in most British supermarkets – you have two alternatives. You can make the passata from tinned tomatoes or you can use simple, ready-made supermarket passata. A warning here: never use other than the *simple* variety. Shy away from anything containing extra ingredients or from ready-made tomato sauces. They are much more expensive and taste worse.

Once you have your passata, you make the tomato sauce as follows. Fry some garlic or chopped onions, add the passata and simmer for about 15-20 minutes, less if you have pre-cooked the tomatoes. When cooking the passata made from fresh or tinned tomatoes do not cover the pan with a lid; this is to allow evaporation and thus end up with a fairly condensed sauce rather than a runny red liquid. The ready-made passata from supermarkets is usually fairly dense and I tend to cover the pan in which it cooks, leaving only a small gap for some evaporation.

Your tomato sauce is then ready to garnish pasta or rice or to use in a variety of dishes. Pasta dishes with any type of tomato sauce should have the final addition of a few fresh basil leaves torn over the serving dish directly. This will release their aroma. Offer grated parmesan cheese to your family and friends.

Cooking pasta

The historian John Dickie traces the introduction of dry pasta into Italy to the Arab conquest before the second millennium. Pasta is best cooked in plenty of boiling water. As a rough guide you need at least one litre of water for 100gm of pasta. As soon as you put the pasta in, add salt and stir. Continue stirring from time to time while keeping the water boiling. Italians do not usually put in drops of oil in the water to prevent the pasta pieces sticking together; we manage the process through stirring. But there is nothing wrong with putting a few drops in if it makes the process easier for you. The cooking time for pasta varies. I usually mistrust so-called quick-cooking pasta. It is often a sign of poor quality because the best pasta takes time to cook unless it is very small or very thin spaghetti. The general rule is: do not overcook. Your pasta must be *al dente* which means that you must feel the bite when you eat it. When you take the pan off the hob put a shot of cold water from the tap into it to stop the cooking process. However, John Dickie reminds us that the modern way of cooking pasta, *al dente*, is at variance with the early serving of this dish. For a long time diners preferred it well cooked. Indeed the 1896 Baedeker to southern Italy recommended British travellers to insist that their macaroni be *ben cotti*, well cooked.

6

Extended family: the 'sweets' side

I dash and sprinkle myself with the bright waters of childhood.
Virginia Woolf

Within my family there was often talk about people who had emigrated or were about to. We children were not much affected by this. My father never contemplated emigration and neither did any of our close relatives. There were two exceptions: one of my younger uncles and my eldest girl cousin, the one who joined, in Australia, the husband she had never met.

My mother's younger brother Pino – Giuseppe – left Delianuova for Hamilton in Canada not for economic reasons but to follow his sweetheart Mela – Carmela. Her family had emigrated taking her along. We all felt sorry when he left. My mother cried for weeks and weeks and my grandfather Antonino took seriously ill. To our eyes, Zio Pino was young, handsome, elegant and dashing. I missed his visits when he entertained us with witty stories. He used to curse our parish priest and his sacristan for ringing the church bells far too early in the morning. Zio Pino's bedroom in my grandfather's house was almost next door to the church of the Assunta. The clanging of bells denied a fair share of sleep to a young man who, naturally, liked to be out and about with his pals late in the evening. When I visited him in Canada many years later I talked to him about this. By then he had become rather nostalgic about the peals of the Delianuova church bells.

One of the real-life stories that Zio Pino was fond of repeating to us and other relatives related to my sister. It pleased me because, for once, my sister emerged as the silly baby. He had come to visit us rather late in the evening. Franco and I were in bed. Angela wanted to stay up and listen to her uncle's stories, but gradually tiredness overcame her. She took off her shoes and fell asleep on the floor. Some time later in the evening, the two adult siblings saw Angela stir, spring up, take down her knickers, pick up one of her shoes, crouch on it and pee.

Zio Pino was one of a family of four boys and three girls. They all married and had several children. So did the nine children on my father's side. As a result I can boast 50 first cousins, 25 on each side. There were also numerous second cousins and great uncles and aunties.

Grandfather Antonino – Nino – Scutellà was the son of a tailor. He owned and managed a café located on the ground floor of his house. A small, timid and neat man, Nonno Nino served graciously the people he thought highly of and in a more off-hand way all the others: the *genti bassi* – the lower classes – and the *genti brutti* – the ugly people. He had different sets of playing cards as well as glasses and cups for the various groups of people, the ones he approved or disapproved of. On one occasion I heard him say that he washed the different crockery with different degrees of care. To a worried daughter he added:

'I am careful when the *genti brutti* are around.'

His son Rocco was a top class *pasticciere* – pastry cook – renowned in the whole region. Trained in Messina, he applied his skills in Delianuova and produced the most exquisite cakes, gateaux, sweets and ice creams. Production of excellent cakes has continued with his son, Nino, and now his grandson Rocco.

Zio Rocco was particularly fussy about the freshness of the ingredients he used in his cakes. He would not use eggs or milk more than a couple of days old. This was one of the reasons why his supply was always well below demand. Another was that he wanted to have a hand in everything produced to ensure cleanliness and quality. To satisfy as many customers as possible, he would cut down each order and gently try to convince his customers that the

5. Nonno Nino in his café

smaller amount he was supplying would be more than sufficient for their needs. I now suspect that Zio Rocco's behaviour towards his customers was part of his general attitude to life. Though very kind and gentle, he was a strict man who did not favour indulgences and luxuries. Had he been living in northern countries he would have made a good Presbyterian. On one occasion well after the war, talking to my mother, he lets out his feelings:

'It is outrageous to walk along the corso and see it littered with chocolate and sweet wrappings. In our younger days it was chestnut peel because that was the only treat children were given. It is a sign of how much parents spoil their children nowadays.'

In fact most of the chocolates and sweets whose wrappings littered the corso came from his shop.

Zio Rocco never ate his own cakes. The only treat for him was special biscuits made occasionally by his older sisters, Zia Maria and my mother. One such occasion was his nameday on 17 August, when we paid two visits: the first one to him to wish him well and to eat his delicious cakes while he ate the inferior ones made by his sisters; the second visit was to the nearby village of Acquaro to enjoy the fair in honour of its patron saint, San Rocco. As my uncle grew old the respect for him in the community increased and on his nameday many people wanted to wish him well. This proved too much for shy Rocco. To escape the fuss he used to disappear into the woods for walks and reflections. Zia Angelina, his wife, received the good wishes on his behalf with her natural grace and bonhomie.

We were all very fond of Zia Angelina, a sensitive and generous non-blood relative. She came from Oppido Mamertina, a small town further down on the plain. It is an area in which there is evidence of civilization well before the arrival of the Greeks. Augusto Placanica, the foremost historian of Calabria, reports the finding of objects from the Iron Age.

In her quiet, unassuming way Zia Angelina had a strong role in the development of her husband's business. She certainly learned the skills very fast and worked full time alongside him. I have been reminded of her by a recent interview in the *Financial Times* of another woman from the same area bearing the same surname: Tripodi. This contemporary, strong Calabrese woman had been mayor of Rosarno. She is one of three Calabrian women mayors who recently dared to take on the local mafia. They go about their lives under *carabinieri* escort. Who knows? There may be some truth in the legend of resolute women and the birth of Locri, a town not far from these localities. This colony is supposed to have been established by Greek women tired of waiting at home for their men to return from their long wars.

It is winter and a quiet week for Zio Rocco and his pastry business. We are invited for lunch at Nonno Antonino's where the cooking is done by Zia Angelina. When we arrive she is still busy adding the finishing touches to cakes and sweets for the business. She also has her cooking going. It is usually *brodo*, meat broth, in which she cooks some small pasta shapes and tiny little meatballs, *polpettine*. Today I arrive early and help her to mince the meat. We use a hand mincer set at the edge of the table. I place a largish piece of meat into the cavity of the mincer, turn the handle and watch streams of curly bits of meat drop into a dish placed on the table. When the mincing operation is complete Zia Angelina prepares the mixture. To the minced meat she adds breadcrumbs, eggs, grated cheese, milk and parsley. I help knead it into a paste. Oh! The pleasure when my hands dip into the soft mixture. Finally I help her to make the *polpettine*.

'... but remember Grazietta, do them very small.'

I get bits of mix on the palm of my left hand, roll them into tiny balls with my right hand and drop them on to a dish.

'... very small, Grazietta, very small.'

The *polpettine* are then dropped into the boiling broth with the pasta. The mixture of tiny balls and small pasta shapes is delicious. I feel proud of my contribution to the roundness and smallness of the balls. In each spoonful I try to identify the very *polpettine* I made before I pop them into my mouth.

These Sunday lunches are also most welcome because we know that there will be a sweet at the end. Zio Rocco always produces something. When nothing is left by the demanding customers, he sets aside for us the crusty edges of the *Pan di Spagna* – bread of Spain – a soft sponge to which he adds some custard. The delicious taste of this mixture has remained with me for years.

The other Scutellà boys took on different professions. Zio Raffaele, Rafeli, the eldest, became a *ebanista*, a refined furniture maker, who moved to Rome when business became scarce with the influx of cheap, ready-made furniture. He made the marital furniture for my parents.

Zio Domenico, Micu, married Zia Fortunata, Nata, when they were both in their teens. They were seen – or so the family story was related to us children – talking together in the countryside. To put an end to gossip, the families agreed they should get married. It was a very successful marriage which gave me seven cousins. Zio Micu managed to learn various trades from barber to wine merchant to travel agent for emigrants. He later moved to Reggio Calabria, mainly to have a better base for educating his children. He took on a job with the council and studied in the evening to acquire a qualification which would allow him to progress.

Zia Maria, the eldest of the three Scutellà girls, married Arcangelo, the town postman, and they had six children. Zio Arcangelo was a keen and gifted musician who played the clarinet and flugelhorn in the Delianuova orchestra. He was part of a strong musical tradition in the town and in Calabria. The orchestra had been established in the late nineteenth century and was known throughout the region. It was disbanded in the 1950s as emigration deprived it of several players and made recruitment difficult. It has recently been revived and Delianuova now boasts one of the best youth orchestras in Italy.

On Tota, the youngest of my Scutellà aunts, more in Chapter 17. I never met my maternal grandmother, Grazia Maglio, after whom I was named. She died of tuberculosis when she was in her early 50s. The family was left distraught and all her children passed on stories of what a wonderful woman she was. I know of one peculiar family relationship involving Nonna Grazia. She always addressed her husband and her grown-up sons with the 'voi' form: the polite, respectful form. Her daughters and young sons were addressed with the informal 'tu'. The celebration of Nonna Grazia's life had a rewarding side for us children for decades after her death. Every year on 18 August, Nonno Nino organized a special remembrance Mass. All the relatives were invited, indeed expected, to participate. After Mass we would gather at his home where Rocco and Angelina treated us to delicious cakes and drinks.

Nonno Nino had one sister, Marianna, and two brothers, Angelo and Agostino, both employed by the city council. All three were alive during the period of these recollections. Zia Marianna's husband had migrated to Australia. He soon stopped all communication and effectively abandoned her and their daughter. She was left very poor and her brothers helped her a little from time to time. She used to do embroidery on commission for people and particularly crochet work, in which she excelled. When aged 90 she heard that I was marrying an Englishman and wanted to make for me her last white bed-spread all in crochet.

All the Scutellà relatives knew that Great Aunt Marianna was a little touchy. She felt that as the eldest female in the clan she was due special respect. She became very offended if, whenever she had even a slight upset, every single one of her relatives, from brothers and their wives to all their children, did not call in to enquire after her health. As soon as a cold or sprained ankle afflicted her, she would send her daughter to inform one of the relatives, expecting the news to spread swiftly and the line of visitors to start.

'Maria, thank you for coming to see me. I think my days are numbered and yet I feel the respect and affection for me waning away. None of my brother Angelo's daughters came. Only he and his wife. And as for your family your husband and sons do not seem to care much for me.'

She always rushed to pay visits to any of her sick relatives and she felt very offended if not informed. Visiting relations and friends was a favourite pastime for women. You could be sure to find other relations and friends at the bedside of the sick person and could thus spend a pleasant afternoon catching up on gossip. Gwen Raverat, granddaughter of Charles Darwin, reports in the memoir of her Cambridge childhood how interest in illnesses was a family characteristic. Her Aunt Etty writes in one of her letters: 'Anybody being ill is like champagne [to me] for the time being.' Zia Marianna is unlikely to ever have tasted champagne but she certainly seemed to have derived as much enjoyment from illnesses as Aunt Etty. Visits to sick people by Zia Marianna could also have a therapeutic purpose. She was an expert healer. Her expertise was often used on me as I will relate later.

Great Uncle Angelo married Rosaria, the sister of my grandmother Grazia. Thus two brothers married two sisters. This was known as a *dubru*, doubling up. Two of the three daughters of Angelo and Rosaria were disabled and my mother used to say it was all the fault of the African wars during which he had picked up nasty infections. He used to talk a lot about his African service and had brought back sea-shells as presents for his relations. A large one was given to my mother and is now sitting on a shelf in the bathroom of my London home.

As a child I was fascinated by both the word and the concept of *dubru*. Doubling up is a practice not unknown in the ancient Greek world from which many Calabrians derive. Helen, of Troy fame, and her sister Clytemnestra married the two kingly brothers Menelaus and Agamemnon. They were not as loved by their wives as Nonno Nino and his brother Angelo. I often wondered whether my sister and I might do *dubru* and marry two brothers in later life. I used to look around for a suitable couple of brothers but could not find any to satisfy me. In the end we did not do *dubru*: she married a Neapolitan, Pasquale, and I an Englishman. Our husbands got on very well and the two families used to spend summers together at Tor San Lorenzo, a seaside resort near Rome. The two brothers-in-law would chat away about politics or science over long lunches, enjoying my mother's Calabrian dishes and the local wine. It all came to an end with Pasquale's death from cancer in 1991.

Calabrian cooking: Zia Angelina's Sunday lunch

Il bollito di Zia Angelina

Bollito – broth – dishes were often used for Sunday lunch on the Scutellà side of the family. They are excellent winter dishes. Traditionally they are also used to strengthen up a convalescing person because they are easy to eat and strong in proteins. An added advantage of the traditional *bollito* is that you are left with meat and vegetables for a second course or an extra meal.

You need a good, solid chunk of meat such as shin of beef. Chicken legs or other chicken pieces can also be used. I tend to remove the skin and any visible fat. Add the following vegetables whole: 1 or 2 carrots, 1 or 2 celery stalks, 1 or 2 large onions, a handful of parsley and a few pieces of skinned ripe tomatoes; tinned tomatoes will do. Put everything in plenty of water and boil till the meat is tender. Skim it from time to time. If you want a very good broth you start with cold water in which you place all your ingredients. If the meat is to be used as a main course then start with boiling water and place the meat and vegetables into it. It takes about one hour of simmering. Try the meat and vegetables with a fork. When ready remove them from the pan, place them on a dish and cut both meat and vegetables – including the onions – into large chunks. Add a few spoonful of very hot broth to keep the meat moist. *Salsa verde* (see Chapter 17) – green sauce – goes very well with *bollito* meat.

For the first course give your family a bowl of *pasta in brodo*. Pass the broth through a sieve to discard the tomatoes, seeds and parsley. Cook the pasta directly in your clear broth. You can use very small pasta such as *conchigliette* or *capelli d'angelo* cut into small pieces. Encourage your diners to add some parmesan cheese after you serve it.

Polpettine di Zia Angelina

Use 300gm of minced lean meat, one egg, about 100gm of bread-crumbs, some grated parmesan, about half a glass of milk, some chopped parsley and salt. Place everything in a bowl and mix with your hands till it becomes a soft but consistent whole. The final mixture should be soft but not runny or crumbly. You can adjust the consistency by adding breadcrumbs – to make it less watery and more consistent – or milk if it is too hard.

You can use the mixture to make a variety of meatball dishes. Zia Angelina – with my enthusiastic help – added tiny meatballs to her broth and pasta. If you do that, the pasta dish becomes a main course. My grandchildren Penelope and Daniel love pasta and *polpettine in brodo*. They also like them cooked in a tomato sauce which is then used to garnish the pasta. For this dish, I prepare meatballs of about 1½cm in diameter. In a shallow oven dish I lay a small amount of tomato sauce at the bottom and then place the meatballs in it as I roll them. I then top them with extra sauce, cover the dish loosely with tin foil and bake at 180 degrees for about 40 minutes. This dish can be used as condiment for pasta or rice.

7

Extended family: bricks, mortar and Hail Marys

'Just think, - to be Solness, the master builder! ... '
'You began as a poor boy from the country - and now,
here you are, the first man in your profession.'
Henrik Ibsen

I got to know both my grandparents on my father's side quite well: Francesco Giuseppe Ietto and Mariangela Leuzzi. I also met her parents. Bisnonno Eugenio Giovanni (Gianni) - Grandma Mariangela's father - was a skilled carpenter. A sweet man, rather small and shrunken in old age, he used to wear an impressive black cape fastened to the shoulder with a golden chain. His wife, Bisnonna Francesca, came from a family of local minor gentry. Her family allowed her to marry beneath them to the man she was in love with and by whom she was much loved. The family agreement was not due to tender feelings towards the two young lovers. Though Mariangela was a great beauty, she was 'a little weak in the head'. She was, therefore, unlikely to attract a husband from the same social background. She became even weaker after her adored only son, Great Uncle Peppino, migrated to Australia. The only child left near her was my grandmother. She, inexplicably, held her daughter responsible for Peppino's departure. She disliked her all her life.

My grandmother loved her mother and looked after her very well. She took her into her home when she became frail and in need of assistance. Bisnonna Francesca lived to a great age and died during the war. I remember everybody crying when she died.

My mother later told me that the laments were not so much for the death of the old great granny but for the penuries and sorrows of the war. She also remembered with gratitude how the sister of a local landowner came to pay a visit of condolence. Seeing the dire situation, the kind lady later sent her maid with some food for the children: the three of us plus the younger of our uncles. The family never forgot that generous gesture and no doubt others. In the years to come the economic tables turned as Italy industrialized after the war. More than 20 years later the generous lady's family was helped by the Ietto brothers to overcome the financial difficulties of decreasing land values and meagre income from its produce.

Bisnonna Francesca was always sweet and patient with us, her great grandchildren, and used to give us treats. She was also fond of our mother. She was graceful and dainty and always elegantly dressed. Some of her old-fashioned, long dresses passed on to my mother and we children used to dress up in them from time to time. At my parents' wedding she wore her best clothes. She squeezed her waist into a tight corset and fitted several layers of skirts and petticoats. Half-way through the party she fainted and it took some time to release her from her clothes and allow her lungs to breath.

The younger uncles used to tease their grandmother and called her Nonna Fancinna, a distortion of her name with connotations of madness.

'Nonna Fancinna, let's dance; let's dance. *La tarantella, la tarantella.*'

Their mother would get very annoyed and chase them away with her broomstick.

Nonna Mariangela was small and pretty in her youth but became fat and slovenly in old age. She was very religious and used to sit for hours reciting the rosary or reading prayers from an old book printed in large characters. She had a very structured and hierarchical view of celestial powers. When you are in trouble and in need, you should pray and ask for divine intervention. However, it is too presumptuous to address yourself directly to God.

'God is too busy. You should not disturb Him. Pray to the Madonna and ask Her to intercede for you with Her son Jesus. A son would never refuse the request of his mother.'

Nonna drew inferences from her own situation in which her eight sons adored her and did their best to please her. But one should not be over demanding of the Madonna either: She has so many causes to plead for. That's where the saints come in. In Nonna's view of the divine world, saints are not as powerful as the Madonna, let alone God, His son Jesus and the Holy Spirit. However, they are specialized and each looks after a particular field. If you are travelling you should invoke the protection of Saint Christopher. If you have throat problems your saint is Nicholas, and so on. She would recommend a specific saint for most human problems and suggest that we address our prayers to him or her as well as to the Madonna to be on the safe side. Never directly to God.

The specialization of saints and madonnas by areas of expertise as well as geography and town is nothing new in Italian Catholicism. For centuries it has encouraged *campanilismo* or civic pride around the town bell-tower. Norman Douglas writes on it with gusto. Feelings of religious *campanilismo* are still present and they are now strengthened by competition around football clubs.

I do not know how Nonna coped with all those children when she was young. I do know how she coped in later years: through the hard work of her only daughter, Antonia - Tota. In the middle of a domestic crisis when the clock was ticking and shirts had to be ironed, meals prepared, washing done, the house cleaned, beds made, Nonna would sit down, take up her prayer book and start invoking divine help. Help did indeed come to her in the shape of Tota rushing around to do all the chores for her parents and brothers.

We children were also often set to work on shopping errands or other small chores. One that grandma was very keen for us to do and we very keen to avoid was an autumnal one: the shelling of butter beans from their pods after they had been dried in the summer sun. According to Nonna this was a very easy task that we could all do while sitting down with her and praying. The shells were hard and small hands got easily tired. As for praying, we felt that we did enough of it in church and at afternoon school. We tried to avoid visiting in the autumn but our efforts were not always successful.

Nonna Mariangela often used to complain about feeling unwell. This meant either that she felt very weak and needed 'substance' in the form of good food, or that she had a tightening in her chest. Her finger pointed to the very spot. This second type of complaint usually gave vent to – and was relieved by – attacks of *sterica* or hysterics. She sat quietly in her chair next to the balcony overlooking Largo Rosario and the corso. Her prayer book was gradually lowered on to her knees. She complained of feeling unwell. Suddenly she would emit a scream so loud as to be heard on the other side of the town. After three or four of these hysterical shouts she declared herself relieved though weak and in need of 'substance'. Tota prepared a soft-boiled egg and some other little treat and all would be well. Our grandma was not the only middle-aged woman to have attacks of *sterica*. Only women seemed to suffer from it and older Deliese people were used to screaming women. The younger generation of Iettos felt uneasy about their screaming mother and one of my uncles suggested shutting the windows during these attacks.

Nonna became very fond of her food. In old age both she and my grandfather kept their own secret store of chocolates locked away from each other and from everybody else. They continued to consider them unaffordable, even as the family grew prosperous. Occasionally they would offer some to us children. We often declined. The chocolates were stale. By the time my grandparents reached old age, sweets were no longer such a rare treat in the family.

Nonna had always been very thrifty, urging Tota to use the last scraps of food or fabric. Men's shirts with worn-out collars were not discarded. Tota replaced the collars first and eventually made underwear out of the less worn part of the material. On one occasion, when I visited as a young woman, Nonna complained that Velia, one of her daughters-in-law, always bought tomatoes at the beginning of the season. They were then quite expensive. Velia explained that they contained vitamins, good for her children. Nonna was not happy:

'Isn't this a waste? Aren't tomatoes just as full of vitamins in late season? Can't one wait another two or three weeks to fill up with vitamins?'

Nonna keenly observed her increasing number of daughters-in-law and became fond of all her grandchildren and followed their progress. She had clear criteria on what made a good woman and a good daughter-in-law. The worst sins were vanity and waste. A woman must not be vain and she must be economical in the running of her household. Nonna also believed that Cupid should be helped. She developed plans for finding suitable marriage partners for her children and grandchildren in which she was largely unsuccessful. She suggested a possible husband for my sister:

'He would be an excellent partner for you. He comes from a good family and is a lawyer. He is a little plump but you should not pay attention to such silly things as appearance.'

Angela replied that she prefered thin men. Unknown to Nonna, she was already in a relationship with the thin man of her life. Nonna tried also with my brother but he too found his own partner. She did not try with me. She thought that I was too difficult a case on account of my bookishness and, of course, the old heart problem.

If not on my married life, Nonna Mariangela had a long-term effect on my time-management skills. For years, in my adult life when I was very busy and making endless lists of chores for home and work, one memorable phrase from her would ring in my ears:

'*Primi e poi primi* (first and then first).'

When things got tough around her and Tota was overwhelmed with work, Nonna from her sitting position and between prayers would look up and pity her daughter. She called her sweet names and told her not to get too worried and to do things roughly and in the correct order.

'*Tota, Totuzza, Totareia*, do not worry. Take things as *primi e poi primi*.'

This was Nonna's time-management rule of unwritten work lists: do the most urgent things first and then pass on to the next one, which in turn becomes the first.

My grandfather Francesco Giuseppe – Ciccio – was known, for miles around, as an excellent builder in terms of skill, honesty and reliability. He was proud of his professional reputation. I heard him say that though he worked with his hands, he never became a journeyman. He had always taken independent work, usually building houses or extensions. The following story was passed on to us. While working in private homes, builders were usually provided with lunch by the lady of the house. On one occasion in a town near Delianuova the woman was generous as well as an excellent cook. The builders decided to enjoy the offering for as long as possible. The works proceeded so slowly that in the end the lady's husband dismissed them and my grandfather got the commission to finish the job.

Nonno's father had been a bailiff to a local landowner. He had died young and none of his grandchildren had known him. But one aspect of his life was passed on to them – his neat and beautiful handwriting. With the death of his father – the only breadwinner in their home – Francesco came under pressure to earn a living for the family which comprised two sisters, Antonia and Domenica.

Francesco was a healthy, strong and handsome young man. Quite early on, he had set his eyes on young Mariangela Leuzzi. But it was not appropriate for him to marry before Antonia and Domenica. Marrying off his sisters to suitable husbands was difficult without a dowry. Skilled though he already was, Francesco found it difficult to secure work and earn enough money, so the only solution was to emigrate. Thus aged 16, he went to the USA. The Ellis Island Foundation records him arriving in New York on 15 May 1909, having travelled on the ship *Luisiana* from Naples. He did not stay long in New York. He disliked *a Merica* and later in life would talk about *Broccolino* and *Broncso* as terrible places. I do not know whether he saved any money. His sisters did marry. Antonia later emigrated to the south of France with her family; Domenica settled in Delianuova.

My father developed a special relationship with his Zia Domenica and her husband. They could not have children, while my grandparents produced one after the other. The two couples lived very close to each other and made an arrangement for the first

6. Nonni Mariangela and Francesco Ietto

born, Pietro, to be raised by Domenica and her husband. It was an informal agreement for the boy, who later became my father, to be cared for and supported by his uncle and aunt. This created deep emotional problems that stayed with my father for the whole of his life. He felt rejected by his own parents and that his rights as first-born had been assumed by his younger brother Eugenio Giovanni (Gianni). At the same time, his brothers were envious that he should get better clothing and food than they. He was seen as the dandy of the family. Throughout his life Papà was always very meticulous about his clothes and shoes and took great care of his appearance. In his more mature years, his suit jacket always sported a pocket square made from a perfectly ironed handkerchief. The tricky fitting was my mother's job. His Sunday shoes always shone. He was very proud of his wavy hair which was still black when he died aged 63. He used to brilliantine it and went to the barber for shaving and hair trimming once a week throughout his life. He was also rather meticulous in his handwriting, which was, largely, in block letters. Did Zia Domenica encourage him to emulate the bailiff grandfather he had never met?

When he married my mother in 1937, Pietro was 24 and his

bride 21. He took her to his uncle and aunt's house from day one. According to Mamma, Zia Domenica was a much worse mother-in-law than Nonna Mariangela. My father loved his aunt and would have liked his second daughter, myself, to be called after her. My mother put her foot down and insisted on me being named after her mother. So I was spared the name Domenica.

Though I never met Great Aunt Domenica and her husband, I have a strong, almost daily association with them in my London home. At some point in their life her husband emigrated to America. He left without mentioning it outside the family. One day he disappeared and his friends and neighbours learned that he had gone to America. He returned a few years later bringing a most impressive trunk which has remained with my family ever since. It has always been known as the *baule americano*, the American trunk. My mother used it to transport her trousseau to Rome when we moved there. Many years later I used it to take my belongings to Boston when I went on a year's study in 1966. When I got married, it was neatly lined and restored to carry my trousseau from Rome to London. My immediate family - Donald, Mark and I - used it to ship our belongings to Boston when we went on a sabbatical term in the summer of 1982. As I write, it sits in my bedroom in London and is full of linen, some unused. I still refer to it as *il baule americano*.

When insisting on naming me Grazia rather than Domenica, Mamma was adhering to the conventional code of practice for the naming of one's children. It was a very strict and invariable rule. The children should be named after their grandparents, starting with the paternal side and then going on to the maternal. My sister was named Angela after Nonna Mariangela, my brother after Nonno Francesco, and I after my maternal granny. In larger families children would be named after other relations: uncles and aunties on the father's side and then on the mother's side. Occasionally, younger children were named after their own parents. Departing from the rule was considered disrespectful and unusual, but it did happen. Zia Maria's husband, the musician postman, insisted on naming his first daughter Aida in honour of Verdi, and, being a monarchist, his second one Elena in honour of the queen of Italy. He was considered an eccentric.

This unwritten rule for naming one's children greatly restricted the range of names available within families and, indeed, in a relatively small society with a considerable number of intermarriages, the restriction applied to the whole of Delianuova and to my extended family. The reader may have already noted that I have mentioned a Zia Tota on both sides of the family. There were also two Zio Raffaeles, Domenicos, Roccos and Angelos. It was possible to differentiate because each name is susceptible to a variety of nicknaming, some made through shortening and some by lengthening the name. Many Italian words can, in fact, be lengthened by adding suffixes. I was called Grazietta. A cousin was Graziella. We needed differentiation of the Grazias as my Scutellà part of the family ended up with no fewer than seven, one for each family. Sometimes we identified a specific Grazia by the name of her Scutellà parent: Grazia di Giulia or di Maria or di Rocco, and so on.

The range of surnames was not that large either. A common surname is Garibaldi. As a teenager studying history I often wondered why. The following possible explanation comes to mind. In 1860 Garibaldi and his thousand fighters, *i mille*, landed at Marsala on the western coast of Sicily, advanced through the island and proceeded via Calabria to the north. They passed through the areas around Delianuova. The great hero of emerging Italy was himself wounded in Aspromonte, very near Delianuova, by the regular army of the king of Piedmont, soon to become the king of Italy. Many years later my uncle Mimmo Ietto showed me with pride the little memorial he had built on behalf of the regional authority. The connection with surnames might be that nine months after *i mille* passed by, there may have been a flurry of births. The new mothers may all have wanted to believe that the great man himself had fathered the children. But all this is pure speculation on my part. It may well be that many families changed their surnames as a sign of their enthusiasm for the hero and his achievements.

The restricted range of first names and surnames may have been responsible for my fascination with surnames as a child. The

surname of a new aunt or uncle gave me the feeling of expanding into a whole new world. I kept repeating over and over again
the whole range of surnames I was connected to: Leuzzi, Pugliese,
Scutellà, Tripodi, Benincasa, Musitano, Caminiti, Musolino,
Strano, Costarella, Stivani. Some even from the north of Italy like
that of my aunt Velia Arduini.

My grandparents had eight sons – Pietro, Gianni, Peppino, Rocco,
Domenico, Angelo, Raffaele and Francesco (or Ciccio) – and one
daughter, Tota. Grandfather Ciccio brought up his children to be
very hard working. He liked to be in control of his family and was
a strict disciplinarian. Occasionally he beat his sons. When one of
them had misbehaved very badly the first question he asked himself
was: will father use a stick, bare hands or the leather belt? The
leather or the buckle side? My grandmother often tried to protect
them with her own body, at which point her husband would stop.
He never beat Tota, but then it is difficult to imagine that he could
have ever found anything to reproach her for. We grew up to fear
Nonno Francesco: just the look of this tall, stern man with a long
and thick moustache intimidated me. In fact, he never raised his
hands to us or even reproached us and was always very gentle with
me.

      None of Francesco's children used violence against their own. I
never remember any of us being beaten by either of our parents. I
do, however, remember my father getting very annoyed if ever my
sister neglected her main duty towards him, which was to buy a
copy of *Il Corriere dello Sport* every Monday from the post office.

      The older Ietto boys learned the building trade from their
father and the younger ones from their brothers. Bright and very
hard working, the brothers quickly developed organizational and
entrepreneurial skills. They had already started little businesses,
in building and in the trading of mica, before the war. They were
aided by the small capital that came to my father through my mother's dowry. The postwar years were very propitious for those skilled
in the technicalities and the organization of the building trade:
the whole of Italy needed rebuilding. They took the opportunity
and started bidding for public contracts within Calabria first and

then moved to Rome, branching out further afield with bigger and bigger contracts.

Nonno Ciccio's original house was on three floors with three bedrooms on the third floor. Later, when economic conditions improved, the house was considerably extended. The brothers acquired the two adjacent houses on each side and made a larger family home. After many years of disuse the enlarged house has recently been gifted to the local church by the numerous grandparents' inheritors. A scouts' meeting house has been established in it.

In the original house there was a balcony off the master bedroom on which Nonno installed a small toilet room. One day he replaced pieces of newspaper with proper toilet paper. A few weeks later during Sunday lunch when most of the family was present he drew our attention to the overuse of toilet paper:

'I have calculated the consumption of toilet paper. We each only need to use it once a day unless we suffer from diarrhoea. I reckon that we are currently using three to four times more than we should. You either change your wasteful habits or I will stop supplying toilet paper.'

All eyes became fixed on the lunch plates. Blushes of guilt rushed to my cheeks. The supply of paper was not stopped. One of the older sons may have had a quiet word with him after lunch.

At the dining table he was always in command, sitting at the head and controlling the flow of food. He particularly liked to be in charge of bread. He expected the large, round loaf to be placed next to him together with his personal kitchen knife. This was used only by him and only for bread. He would cut the bread and hand out slices at our request. He used to get very annoyed if anyone placed the bread on the table upside down, the flat side up, or in any offhand manner: bread had to be treated with consideration and respect.

The culinary standard of Sunday lunch at the Iettos was not great. We usually had pasta and ragù. Tota would later display excellent culinary skills but in these early days she was too busy with other chores to devote her full attention to cooking. One Sunday the stew overcooked while she attended to her mother. When her sisters-in-law appeared keen to help, the situation often got worse. Pasta salted by more than one sister-in-law was not uncommon.

For us children, it was good to have so many uncles and aunties. We hardly saw the men on weekdays. But on Sundays, as we walked to church or joined our friends for games, they were all around and we would go up to them to say hello. We often received a few cents for a Sunday treat: *a fera*. On the whole I have fond memories of my extended family on both the Scutellà and Ietto sides. But, looking back, I see snippets of more problematic relationships between uncles, aunts and their nieces. A little girl told us how she avoided one of her uncles because he wanted to touch her. Another girl, older than us, tall and rather ugly-looking, mentioned two extraordinary things about an aunt of hers. The said aunt gave her advice on how to deal with constipation: beat your fists on your knees while sitting or crouching to defecate. The other thing was that the aunt did 'things' with her in bed. However, the niece was reassured by the aunt that what they did was not a sin: 'only what you do with men is a sin'. So there was no need to confess to the priest.

Calabrian cooking: Sunday lunch at the Iettos

Sunday lunch at the Ietto grandparents was a less exquisite experience than the one provided by Zia Angelina at the Scutellàs' home. After the war, when meat became available, *pasta alla Napoletana* or *pasta con ragù* was the standard Sunday fare.

But alas! No sweets were available at the Iettos. A piece of fruit ended the meal. In winter we would have oranges, mandarins, apples or chestnuts. In summer, fresh figs were a favourite dessert with everybody. Norman Douglas in his travels is told by a small boy how Calabria has a very large variety of figs with distinct names. I am afraid I can only recall two types, both delicious: black and white or rather with dark purple or green peel. But I can confirm the second part of the conversation between Douglas and the Calabrian boy. The fig tree is *innamorato delle pietre e cisterne* ('in love with stones and cisterns') which Douglas interprets to mean 'that its roots are searchingly destructive to masonry and display a fabulous intuition for the proximity of water'.

Pasta alla Napoletana

Lightly fry a chopped onion and then add minced meat. Stir and let it brown. Add half a glass of wine - preferably red - and let it evaporate at high temperature. Add tomato passata and bring to the boil. Then turn down the heat and let it simmer for about 30 minutes. Use it as a condiment to whatever type of pasta you like, spaghetti or rigatoni. Add torn basil leaves and sprinkle parmesan cheese before serving.

Pasta con ragù

Ragù is a thick tomato sauce with stewed meat in it. You can use beef or pork or - my favourite - lamb. Place a chopped onion, the meat pieces and a small amount of oil in a stewing pan. Fry at high temperature, turning the meat pieces until brown on all sides. Add half a glass of red wine and let it evaporate. Add passata and bring to the boil. Turn down the heat and let it cook slowly. The cooking time depends on the size and type of meat. Use the ragù as sauce for pasta. It is also very good with rice.

I give here two other pasta dishes, though they were not part of the Iettos' Sunday lunch menu. Like those presented above, they use tomato sauce.

Pasta al forno

This is an excellent dish for a large party. Most pasta dishes require cooking pasta while your guests are having a drink that you cannot share with them. However, this dish can be prepared beforehand, leaving you free to attend to your guests. Use *pasta corta* - smallish type of pasta such as *rigatoni* or *penne* - allowing some 50gm per person. Cook it for a couple of minutes less than the recommended time. Drain and dress the pasta with tomato sauce. You can use *napoletana* sauce which contains meat. If you want a vegetarian dish use simple tomato sauce. Place a small amount of sauce at the bottom of an oven dish and then place a layer of pasta followed by a layer of cheese. Use hard mozzarella cut into small pieces or grated mild cheddar; also add some grated parmesan. Top up with tomato sauce. Then make another layer of pasta, cheese and sauce. The top layer should be of pasta and sauce only. Bake in the oven at 200 degrees for about 40 minutes. I usually cover it loosely with foil for some 30 minutes and remove it for the last ten minutes to give it a little crust. Sprinkle with torn basil leaves before serving.

Penne all'arrabbiata

I am not sure where this delicious dish got its name of 'penne ... in an angry mood'. I venture to suggest that the rough, quick and peppered way of cooking hints at a cook in a not very serene mood. Or it could be that this hot dish is likely to be eaten in a hurry by a person who is likely to become angry ... if distracted from it.

In a large frying pan lightly fry a chopped onion. Add some chilli and fresh – or tinned – tomatoes roughly cut. Add bacon cut into small pieces; I tend to discard the the fatty part. Let the mixture cook for a few minutes. Meanwhile cook your *penne* but leave it a little on the hard side. After draining add to the frying pan, mix all the ingredients and let them cook for a minute or so.

8

The Church

Two nights before the first communion, Father Antonio Isabel
closeted himself with him [Jose' Arcadio Segundo] in the sacristy
to hear his confession with the help of a dictionary of sins.
Gabriel Garcia Marquez

What should I confess? Aged less than nine, this was the first problem in my relationship with 'the Church' and 'the religion'. There
was only one Church and we all belonged to it. A few people were
known to be critical of the Church. They were socialists.

My first confession was prior to receiving Holy Communion for
the first time. Angela, I and many cousins and friends were being
prepared spiritually for this big event in our life. Pious young ladies
gave us catechism lessons and taught us prayers. They introduced
us to the meaning of sin, confession and absolution. We were told
of two types of sin. First there are the mortal ones in which the
offence is so grave that your soul is in danger of eternal death and
for which you would forever burn in hell. These included murder,
theft, stealing other peoples' wives or husbands and fornication. It
was not made clear to us what fornication was and nobody asked.
It could be that the older children knew already and the younger
ones like me were too embarrassed by their ignorance to ask the
question. Sins in this category I had not committed. I was sure of
that.

Then there were the venial sins, the minor ones, which do not
destroy your soul but must nevertheless be confessed. All sorts of

things seem to come into this category: lying, cheating, gossiping, quarrelling, using foul language. Sins can be committed not only in deeds but in thoughts. If a foul word or disrespectful thought came to mind, that was a sin.

I felt under pressure. I had to come up with some sins to confess because that's what confession was all about.

If I cannot find any sin to confess, will they think I am too childish for first Communion?

Following consultation with my mother I decided to list recent quarrels with my brother and sister as genuine sins. I could also include lies among my sins. So that was sorted out. But another problem arose. We were told that confession and penance would clear our souls from sin and it was only in such a clear state that we could receive the body of Christ. For our priest, confession was a big undertaking in the month of May, the First Communion period. All children approaching First Communion had to be confessed, as well as their parents and relations. The priest started this demanding job well in advance. I went to confession a couple of days prior to Communion. My penance was the recitation of a number of Hail Marys and Our Fathers in a contrite state. If I wanted to receive Communion in a pure state, I had to make sure not to commit any more sins in the next two days.

During those two days foul words and disrespectful thoughts kept coming to mind in the form of:

Oh! I must not say or think this or that.

In forbidding myself to think about foul words, was I actually thinking about them? Was this a sin? Had I recited my penances in a really 'contrite' state? Was I impure and not in a fit state to receive Communion? Other children had similar doubts. Quite a few of us went back to confession. The priest looked increasingly exhausted and irritated. He suddenly emerged from the confessional:

'Just go away, all of you children. If you think you may have sinned say a few extra prayers as a penance. Do not come back for confession.'

I spent a very agitated and sleepless night. The next day, First Communion day, all was well: I felt lovely and important in my immaculate long dress and enjoyed the fuss and presents.

On Sundays there were three Masses in our parish. The first Mass at 6am was traditionally considered to be for old women: *pe' vecchi*. The second one was for married and busy women: *pe' maritati*. The last one at 11.30 was, allegedly, for the less serious ones, *pe' spostati*: for children and for young people who wanted to be seen and see others in their best clothes. Some old women went to all three. It was fun and useful. They would get the chance to see most of the parish people and would acquire more indulgences in the life to come.

Angela, Franco and I went to the last one. After our Sunday baths, we put on our best clothes and off we went by ourselves. Mamma had already been to the 8.30 Mass and Papà, already out meeting his friends, might join in for the late Mass.

The men would stand in the piazza outside the church talking and eyeing the young women as they proceeded in their best dresses, shoes and kerchiefs. They were indeed in a key position to scrutinize the arrival of young women along the two sides of the corso as well as from minor small roads all converging on the piazza. The women were stared at by numerous eager eyes as they arrived at the piazza, climbing up the steps from the lower part of the piazza on to the opening in front of the church. Some girls had their heads already covered with a light kerchief. Others paused and put theirs on before entering the church. This created a further opportunity to be admired by their special sweethearts waiting in the piazza. Not all the staring eyes from men were unwelcome. The more daring girls might even throw their own glances at their beloved ones. They had all spent a long time in front of the mirror trying on dresses and shoes and perfecting their walking demeanour. The choice of headcover was one of the essentials. What was most becoming: lace, silk or cotton? Dark or bright colour? Single colour or patterned? They had to get it right. It was the only opportunity during the week to be seen by eager young men.

The priest would position himself at the entrance to the church. He was kind and popular, though known to be irascible and prone to outbursts. He was particularly strict on sexual mores. From this key position he welcomed the congregation while checking the propriety of dress and behaviour. No short sleeves or low-neck dresses were allowed. Heads had to be covered. No woman dared disobey these rules and risk the wrath of God's servant in front of everybody. We little girls could wear short-sleeved dresses but not sleeveless ones.

After the last of the three bell calls, the men would enter the church, the last group to do so. They uncovered their heads before entering the house of God. I was baffled:

'Mamma, when they go into the church, why do women have to cover their heads while men have to take off their hats and caps?'

'Because the priest says so.'

'Why does he say so?'

'I do not know. I think the pope tells him so. You know the pope lives in Rome and he decides what we should or should not do.'

The congregation sat in the order specified by the priest: the children and some old women in the first rows. The old women kept an eye on boisterous children. Other women occupied the middle rows. The men stood at the end. Some older or frail men could sit in the last rows. This congregational arrangement made sure that no contact or communication took place between the sexes.

Not long after my first Communion I experienced my first disenchantment with the Church hierarchy and its operations. It was Passion Week, the week before Easter, and we children were given special instructions. This particular year the priest encouraged us to recite as many *Viae Crucis* as possible. To complete a *Via Crucis* we had to go around the stations of the Cross in the church and recite a prayer in front of each of them. He gave us each a little piece of paper on which to note down our names and the total number of *Viae Crucis* recited. I set to the task with great eagerness and efficiency and completed a very large number which I duly noted down. On the appointed day, the priest collected the papers and we waited for his comments. When it came to mine he looked at me and said:

'Too many *Viae Crucis* are recorded here. You cannot have done them with devotion and attention.'

He gave the prize to a boy who had recited fewer than me. I felt cheated. Nobody had mentioned devotion and attention at the beginning. I did what was requested of me, came first but was denied the prize. I had a lingering suspicion that the fact that I was a girl and the winner a boy had something to do with it.

There were, however, positive sides to being involved in the Church. On Sunday afternoons, after a few prayers and devotions, we were allowed to play on the large terrace above the sacristy. Girls only. The boys played outside. It was possible to borrow books from a sparse, largely religious library. Apart from the school text-books these were the only books we had access to. The church also provided great fun for both adults and children during its religious festivals.

Mamma Giulia's cooking: soups for cold nights

Mamma used to cook thick vegetable-based soups in winter and summer. The summer ones were made with fresh vegetables such as runner beans or cauliflower (see Chapter 3). In winter she used pulses and, in particular, butter beans which were abundant in Calabria even in the war years. They were laid to dry in the summer sun and were thus preserved for the winter months. These were the ones Nonna Mariangela wanted us to shell. I now make these soups regularly in London. On one occasion a British guest described it as a 'lovely vegetable and pasta stew'. They are particularly good on a winter evening and small amounts of chilli on them may further help to fight the cold weather.

Pasta e fagioli

You can use butter beans or borlotti or cannellini beans or a mixture of all three. If you use the dried variety you must follow the instructions for soaking them in water. You can also use pre-cooked tinned beans, though they are not as good as the dried ones. You also need tomatoes, one large carrot, a small amount of celery, pasta, oil and garlic.

Prepare a sauce by frying the garlic, adding tomatoes and finely chopped carrot and celery. Simmer till tender but not fully cooked. As for the beans, when I use tinned ones I sieve half of them in a moulinette. You may avoid this operation if you do not mind quite a lot of bean skin in your soup. Use the bean juice – adding some extra water if necessary – during the sieving. Add the bean paste and the extra beans to the sauce.

Separately, cook some pasta of medium to small shapes. Incidentally this is the traditional dish in which all the remaining bits of dry pasta you may have in your pantry can be used together to good taste and aesthetic effect. If your assorted pasta requires different cooking times, you have to place them into the boiling water at different times.

When the pasta is two or three minutes from full cooking, pour some of its liquid into a bowl and keep aside. Add the pasta and some of its water to the mixture of sauce, paste and beans and finish the cooking. Before serving add some extra oil. Your soup should be left to rest for some ten minutes before serving. It should be rather thick, not too liquid. This dish is also delicious the next day and I always make sure to have enough left over for another meal. Any extra pasta water can be used the next day as well.

The same process can be followed to prepare lentil or chickpea dishes. They both go very well with rice as well as with pasta. Their cooking times are different from that of beans.

Pasta e piselli

Mamma prepared this during the summer when fresh peas were available. We used to help her pod them with great pleasure. They were soft and moist on the skin of our fingers.

Lightly fry a chopped onion and then add the peas with a very small amount of water. Simmer, adding a little more water from time to time. Meanwhile cook your pasta. *Conchigliette* – small shells – are very good for this dish because they often trap a pea inside them. When almost ready, drain some of the pasta water and keep it aside. Add the peas and onions to the rest of the pasta and let them cook together for a couple of minutes. Add more pasta water and oil if you think it necessary.

I now use frozen peas and prepare this dish from time to time all year round. The procedure is more or less the same as above except that you thaw the peas before adding them to the fried onion. Recently I developed a slightly different version of this dish. In a frying pan with a very small amount of oil, I fry the onions and add the peas in their frozen state. I let them cook for a few minutes and then add to the pasta and its water. Both versions taste good. Cooking the peas in a small amount of oil - with or without the onion - has the advantage of keeping all their flavour and goodness in, rather than dispersing it in boiling water.

9

Religion and its festivals

'– Christmas-time! Christmas-time!' said Gabriel, almost trotting to the stairs ... A fat brown goose lay at one end of the table and at the other end, on a bed of creased paper strewn with sprigs of parsley, lay a great ham, stripped of its outer skin and peppered over with crust crumbs, a neat paper frill round its shin and besides this was a round of spiced beef.

James Joyce

Religion regulated family, social and public life. The calendar year was marked by religious festivals. Each brought us a wealth of social gatherings and was celebrated with special food. We also had name-day celebrations which were considered far more important than birthdays. We each had a saint to protect us. If no saint with our name was to be found in the calendar, parents resorted to named madonnas. Failure to well-wish and celebrate with friends and relations on their nameday caused great offence. And you could not claim ignorance as with birthdays – the Church gave you full information about the major saints or you could ask around about the names of minor saints or use your own initiative. The names of saints and madonnas were also listed in the calendars available at public places. When visiting your barbershop, café or grocery all you had to do was look at the list of saints for that particular week or ask somebody to read it for you if you were illiterate.

Nonno Antonino had a curious feature in common with Antonio Gramsci, the political philosopher and activist, though I am sure they did not know of each other's existence nor are they likely to have shared anything else. They had the same nameday. Moreover, they both insisted that the Saint Anthony who was supposed to protect them was not the well-known St Anthony of Padua, whose day was celebrated on 13 June, but St Anthony l'Abbé celebrated on 17 January. Nonno Nino would take offence if the good wishes were given on the wrong St Anthony's day. He felt that people had not bothered to find out who his true patron saint was. Gramsci wrote from jail a humorous reproach to his sister-in-law Tania for sending *auguri* (best wishes) on the wrong St Anthony's day.

My nameday is 2 July, the day of the *Madonna delle Grazie*. It is celebrated in the parish of Pedavoli whose church of San Nicola houses a wooden statue of this particular madonna. For the Scutellà side of the family the celebrations had a special significance because of my maternal grandmother's name. During my childhood there were four Grazias in this side of the extended family living in Delianuova. On our nameday, we and our families would congregate in one of our houses to celebrate. The cakes were happily provided for the occasion by Nonno Antonino and Zio Rocco.

All or most celebrations had a religious connotation. There was no special celebration for New Year. The first big festivity of the year came with Carnival, the week before Lent. There were dances, displays of floats and two special foods: *nnacatole* and *crispelle*. The former are long, thin strips of egg dough. When deep-fried, the strips turn and twist into shapes to be sprinkled with sugar. Some of the shapes suggested to me stories about animals and monsters. The *crispelle* consist of a fried batter mixture stuffed with either savoury or sweet bits.

One carnival, celebrations brought with them disgrace and tears. A younger cousin of my mother became very upset. So did many Deliese girls. On the night of Shrove Tuesday a grand ball was organized in the local *Circolo*. Many young men and women attended. The latter were duly chaperoned. They took part in some modern dances such as the tango and the waltz as well as the traditional *tarantella*. In the latter dance there is no body contact or proximity. In the former there is. The following Sunday the priest gave a blistering sermon on these new, sinful dances, on the decline

of morals, the wickedness of young people and the deterioration of
the watchfulness of their elders. It sent shivers down young and old
spines alike.

Not much seemed to have changed in the relationship between
Calabrese women and the Church in a hundred years. Edward
Lear was rambling through the Aspromonte area in the summer
of 1847 and his diary for 21 August reports that during a religious
festival a public dance in the small town of Gerace near the Ionian
coast was to have been performed by men only. The bishop had
issued a written prohibition on the participation of women.

San Giuseppe, Saint Joseph, was celebrated on 19 March with
Zio Rocco's *bignè* (cream puffs/profiteroles). Soon it was time to
prepare for Easter. During Passion Week special functions were
organized every evening. Preachers came from outside the parish,
though, mercifully, their sermons were for adults only. There was
singing, in which we all participated. I greatly enjoyed the doleful
singing of old women. Heads bent, elbows on their knees, rosa-
ries in their hands, they seemed to put all their sorrows into their
voices. Sometimes the words were in Latin. Nobody seemed to
mind not understanding their meaning. Then there were preparations for the procession. Together with many other girls Angela and
I dressed as angels. Costumes and wings were dug out of the old
sacristy cupboards weeks in advance for restoration work.

We all had to confess and take Communion on Easter Day.
While women were used to weekly confessions, many men would
go for much longer periods without purging their sins. Easter was
the time we all had to do it. Extra priests were set on duty to hear
it all. Men and women were assigned different time slots, just in
case close proximity might have elicited extra sins of thought if not
deed. Nonna wanted to make sure that her boys did the decent
thing:

'Petrantoni, Gianni, Rroccu, Peppino, Angelo ... do not forget
to go to confession. God is merciful and will forgive your sins but
not if you do not purge your soul at Easter.'

They all told her that they had confessed. Possibly one or two
added the sin of lying to their others.

On Easter Day there were long queues for Communion and

men went first. The girls and women enjoyed watching the procession of men in meek and contrite demeanour. For once their stares were on the floor rather than on women. When joining the Ietto grandparents at their home, we children, and often the older members of the family as well, crowned the general feeling of goodness by asking our grandparents to bless us. We lightly bowed in front of them and kissed their hands. They blessed us with a pat on the head. This ceremony became increasingly embarrassing for everybody and was eventually dropped.

Before the food feast, penance had to come in the way of meatless Good Friday. This was hardly a problem in the lean, war years when meat was very scarce. When prosperity arrived, many people had a more liberal attitude to what they ate and when. My father ate anything on Fridays except this one day a year. He did not want to touch any meat on Good Friday. At the beginning of Passion Week he would remind my mother:

'Giulia, remember no meat this Friday. I do not want to commit this grave sin.'

'What nonsense I have to hear. As if there had ever been meat on our table on Good Friday. You take care of your other sins and don't worry about this one.'

Then came the feast. Easter Day was celebrated with home-made egg pasta, lamb or baby goat and two special types of sweets. The first was home-made *gute*, a pastry rolled into a long piece of about 2cm diameter. It was then patterned as a small braid. Between the crossing over of the two sides of the braid an egg was placed. Two thin strips of pastry were laid across the egg to form a cross and hold it in position. The *guta* was now ready for baking. One, two or three egg *gute* were produced and assigned to a child, woman or man. I found this a very unsatisfactory treat: I was never sure whether it was a savoury or a sweet. I liked the pastry but, when breaking my *guta*, some bits of egg shell would mix with it and spoil my pleasure.

The second type of sweet was much more delicious: Zio Rocco's renowned *dita di Apostolo*. Apostles' toes are sweet cannelloni made of thin sponge and filled half with vanilla and half with chocolate custard. Rocco's grandson continues the tradition and produces the same high-quality *dita di Apostolo*. There is another reminder of Apostles' feet, one connected with drama rather than food. One public ceremony was the live re-enactment of Christ washing the Apostles' feet. On a raised platform inside the church, 12 men dressed as Apostles sat on stools while the priest went around and washed their feet.

Have they cleaned their feet before coming to church? Maybe they did not. What is the point, the priest is going to wash them anyway.

My curiosity remained unsatisfied. The platform was too high and I was unable to be close enough to the Apostles to inspect their feet.

On 1 November, the Day of the Dead, Delianuova did not exactly celebrate but we children still had a good time. It was a day off school. In groups of friends and family, we all walked to the Pedavoli end of the town. The old cemetery was outside the inhabited area, not far from a gorge with a charming rivulet. Its entrance had an impressive wrought-iron gate. The tombs were made attractive by marble stones with the names of the dead and their photographs. Some were monumental and had statues or columns to grace the resting place of whole families. The adults made their tomb visits while we amused ourselves with our own friends and watched with interest the outpouring of emotions. Small family refreshments usually followed back home.

Preparations for Christmas started well ahead of time. The *zampognari* – bagpipe players – came from the mountains dressed in their traditional shepherd costumes. They played at street corners and waited for offerings of food and money. They were never disappointed, as everybody enjoyed their performances. The church ladies organized plays with the children as actors. They usually took place in a disused church towards the end side of Paracorio. I was very keen to participate but the time of the year and the excitement did not help. One year I developed a high fever and my part was cancelled. The year after I recited my Christmas poem with a hoarse voice.

Christmas Eve was celebrated with a large *di magro* – non-meat – meal. It was usually *stoccufissu/baccalà*. We were sent to buy a large piece from a fat lady at the other side of the town. At midnight, after the feast, we all went to Mass. There was not a fixed menu for Christmas Day. Most families had a pasta dish followed by meat. On the sweets side there was Zio Rocco's *torrone*, nougat made of almonds and honey and sometimes covered with chocolate. He also made delicious *torrone gelato* made of nougat, sugar and pieces of glacé fruit. *Pignolata* was made of small pastry balls stuck together by a honey mixture and covered with chocolate. All homes had plenty of dried figs often served with walnuts. Both fruits are plentiful. Fig trees were seen everywhere in Delianuova, often growing in courtyards against walls. The figs were dried on shallow baskets during the summer and thus preserved for the winter.

The biggest religious festival was – and still is – Ferragosto for the celebration of the Madonna of the Assumption in the parish church of Paracorio. After the war, the Deliesi wanted to stage a memorable festival on this special day. They still do. The event falls on 15 August at the height of the summer and during the holiday period. Many *forestieri* or *villeggianti* – outsiders or holiday makers usually from Reggio or Messina – used to come and enjoy the cool of the Aspromonte hills during the hottest weeks of the year. In the 1950s and 1960s some of the emigrants made sure to return home for Ferragosto if at all possible. Those who could not return often sent money to the organizing committee as their contribution to a successful festival.

Preparations would start well in advance. Traders arrived from afar and set up their stands with attractions for children and adults. Our uncles gave us pocket money, *a fera*, to be spent at the fair. Mamma always prepared her most delicious dish, *melanzane ripiene*, stuffed aubergines. Zia Velia cooked her northern dish, *mille foglie*. The two sisters-in-law continued to prepare these delicacies for many more Ferragosto festivals after the families moved to Rome. Nonno Ciccio bought the biggest watermelon on the market and left it to cool under a trickle of running water. At the end of the meal, Nonno's watermelon was placed on a large dish in front of him. He sliced it slowly and carefully. Every slice should have a piece of the centre crown, *a curuna*, to ensure that we all had a piece of the best part of the fruit. He encouraged us children to eat as much as we wanted, far more than our mother judged healthy. He watched us all with delight.

In the late afternoon most of us took part in the procession. The statue of the Madonna of the Assumption was taken through Paracorio and along the main road to the second parish church. It was set on a platform supported by long wooden boards. These would sit on the shoulders of several, strong young men on each side. They walked slowly and were replaced by fresher youths along the path. Immediately behind the statue walked the clergy followed by the local *carabinieri* and notables. Then came the ordinary men followed by women and children. Balconies were festooned with displays of the best family bedspreads as decorations. The corso lit up with colours. During the procession banners were raised for people to pin money on from their balconies and windows. The Delianuova orchestra accompanied the statue and in the evening played in the piazza in front of the Church of the Assumption on a purpose-built platform. At night multicoloured fireworks, with louder bangs than we children could ever make, crowned it all.

One year we were told that there was going to be cinema: a new marvellous entertainment just arrived from *a Merica*. We did not know what to expect. No one seemed to know what cinema was. A huge, white sheet was placed on the wall of one of the houses in the piazza. At dusk, people brought chairs and stools and settled down waiting for darkness and the start of the film. We children whiled away the time with games. When the film eventually started I could not understand what was going on. I was overwhelmed by the huge images on the screen. The last sight before I fell asleep on my mother's lap was of the head of a beautiful woman with dark, wavy hair: Rita Hayworth in Gilda? Her smile and soft voice lulled me to sleep. The next day Angela rubbed it in:

'It was fantastic. All the little ones like you fell asleep and missed it.'

Mamma Giulia's cooking: the Ferragosto feast

Melanzane ripiene

Stuffed aubergines was one of my mother's masterpieces. She would only do it once a year for the Ferragosto festival, to 'keep the tradition alive' as she put it. Since her death in 2003, I have started this tradition in my London home. In Delianuova hardly a home would be without *melanzane ripiene* for lunch on 15 August, Assumption Day.

It is not a dish for lazy cooks, I'm afraid. I followed Mamma's recipe during our Rome period. Her preparations started a week or two before, when she would order from her trusted greengrocer special aubergines: fresh and small, the smallest possible among the full-grown ones. The quantity varied according to how many of the enlarged family would join us. There have been years when we were holidaying at the seaside resort of Tor San Lorenzo in which some 30 family members were catered for. We all expected her masterpiece.

A couple of days before Ferragosto she made sure to have all the required ingredients: minced meat; grated parmesan cheese, breadcrumbs and eggs. The day before she prepared the tomato sauce: a lot of it from fresh San Marzano tomatoes. On the actual day she got up early. By the time we emerged from our bedroom, the kitchen was full of activity.

Now for the actual process. Remove the stalks but not the peel from the aubergines and cut them in half lengthwise. Then remove from each half a good deal of inner pulp to leave a hollow boat-like shape. Be careful not to pierce the boat when removing the pulp. Cut the pulp into small pieces (about 2cm cubed) and place them in boiling water for some ten minutes – till very tender – and then toss them into a colander and let them drain and cool down.

Meanwhile you will have a big pan of boiling water in which you blanch the aubergine boats for a couple of minutes. Take them out of the pan with a large spatula. Be careful not to break them. Place them peel-side up on a cloth which you have pre-laid on a smooth surface and let them lose some of the water. When they have cooled down remove them from the – now – wet cloths and turn them up on a flat surface.

Return to your aubergine pulp. Put it in a large bowl and add the minced meat, egg(s), breadcrumbs, grated parmesan and finely chopped parsley. Mix for a few minutes with your hands. You may need to add a small amount of water; the actual amount depends on how much water is retained by the aubergine pulp. Do not add milk. The aubergines will soften the meat mixture. Sprinkle with salt, cover and let it rest for a while. For six aubergines (12 'boats') you may need: 200gm of lean double minced meat, one egg, approximately 100gm of breadcrumbs, a small amount of grated parmesan and, of course, the aubergine pulp. The final mixture should be soft but not runny or crumbly. You can adjust the final consistency by adding breadcrumbs – to make it less watery and more consistent – or water if it is too hard. Fill the aubergine boats with the mixture.

The aubergine boats are now ready for the next stage of the processing: frying in a large frying pan with about 1cm of oil. This is a delicate and dangerous job. I do not recommend it for people who are not old hands at frying. Both sides must be fried and this requires care when turning them face down so as not to separate the stuffing from the aubergine boat. I use two spatulas with long handles to make sure that my hands, arms and face are well out of the range of any oil that may spit out of the pan. It only takes about two minutes on each side. When taken out of the frying pan they must be placed on fat-absorbing kitchen paper and patted on the top side with more paper.

Now for the last stage. Place the aubergine boats in a shallow oven dish in which you have spread a thin amount of tomato sauce. Put a very generous amount of hot tomato sauce on each boat. Cover loosely with foil and bake for about 30 minutes at 200 degrees. Any leftovers can be stored in the fridge but not for more than 2–3 days.

I know this sounds quite daunting but do not despair. I have recently developed an alternative method to my mother's. It is less labour-intensive and the finished dish contains fewer calories. It is also less dangerous as it skips the frying stage. Blanch the aubergine boats in boiling water, let them drip upside down and then stuff them with the pulp mixture. Place them into your oven dish with the tomato sauce underneath and on top of them. Bake at 200 degrees for about 40 minutes.

Both methods result in tasty dishes. I confess that the second one – my innovation – is not as tasty as my mother's more complex method. However, it is much easier and less dangerous to prepare. In London I like to serve the aubergine boats with rice and an extra vegetable such as peas.

10

Fun and play

L'IGNOTA: '... Mi faccia il piacere di parlarmi di me bambina.
Ero così' tanto un'altra, che mi pare, se ci penso, di sognare.'
BOFFI: 'Ma a tutti ormai pare così la vita di prima, signora Cia!'

THE UNKNOWN: '... Please tell me of myself as a child. I was such
a different person, that, when I think of it, I feel I am dreaming.'
BOFFI: 'But that is how our earlier life appears to all of us,
signora Cia!'
Luigi Pirandello

Ferragosto was a special time for enjoyment, but we children had
fun all year round. With the help of grown-ups we made rag dolls.
We used stones and sticks to build little houses and play at families. Around Christmas we played games with nuts or chestnuts of
which there were plenty.

There were more energetic games. Boys played football. There
were always enough cousins and friends around to make two sides.
Some girls like my sister were allowed and indeed encouraged
to join in. I did not dare to ask. A favourite game with all the
Deliese children was cowboys and Indians. Some of my cousins on
the Scutellà side were at an advantage here. Zio Arcangelo – Aunt
Maria's musical husband – in his work as a postman had free access
to unwanted comics. He made them available to his six children
and all their cousins. It was delightful to read the adventures of
Tony Boy, Calamity Jane, Bill Texas, Buffalo Bill and other heroes

of the Wild West. We discussed them at great length, taking the side of our favourite character. We enacted their adventures. I liked to play Calamity Jane: the girl as strong and clever as men. Guns were easily made from sticks or mimicked from our own hands. We needed two sides. I was allowed to play, though each side gently hinted that I should join the other. I joined whichever side I felt like at the moment and sometimes changed sides in the middle of the game. Nobody took any notice.

These games always ended up with quarrels and with everybody accusing the others of cheating. If shot dead, you were supposed to lie flat and stop fighting. But where was the fun in that? Everybody wanted to continue shooting to the end of the game or rather till we were called in by our mothers. The boy or girl who shot somebody always claimed to have shot first and to have hit the heart. But how was one to know who shot first? How did we know where the bullet was lodged? The victim always denied serious damage. I was at times asked to adjudicate the outcome. I did not like this task. It always ended up with resentment against me from some of my cousins. Occasionally I managed to pacify the warring factions by proposing new adventures from the stories in my favourite comics.

I loved reading them. It was almost the only reading material we had. I used to make up for the lack of fictional material by creating my own. Hearing a tale or reading a comic ignited my fantasy and I then spent the next few days weaving my own stories. In them, I was always a grown-up heroine. Tall, blonde, beautiful, strong and intelligent, I was skilled at all trades and professions of both the feminine and masculine varieties. This fantasy, grown-up Grazia went to the rescue of people in trouble. She always managed to emerge victorious by using her exceptional manual, physical and intellectual skills. With great dexterity she rode her white horse through forests, rivers, mountains and cities. Her beauty attracted several young men eager to marry her. She procrastinated.

While weaving my stories I became totally immersed and cut myself off from the real environment. During such episodes of total absorption I would incline my head to one side and turn it slightly upward. Angela and Franco used to tease me for this posture. If they were annoyed with me – usually for being the recipient of my mother's favours – they would remove themselves some distance and shout:

'*Guarda-in-cielo; guarda-in-cielo*'. The one who looks at the sky.

The distance was well advised. I was usually rather meek with them and, on the whole, they were very gentle towards me. But this was the one issue on which I would lose my cool. Their teasing made me furious and I would throw at them whatever was to hand. My fantasies were my own little secret and my head posture was the only external sign of them. I considered fantasizing an embarrassing weakness of which I felt ashamed. My siblings' teasing made me feel exposed to the possible discovery of my secret life.

My daydreaming continued well into my teens and early 20s. My stories evolved according to my age, development and real-life experiences. As a child and, later, as a teenager and young woman, there were times when I felt a great desire, a yearning to fantasize undisturbed.

The building of sewers in Delianuova gave us the opportunity to develop innovative strategies for our cowboys and Indians games. While excavating, the contractors, that is my father and his brothers, left lots of large pipes along the streets. We used them for hide-and-seek games. Years later on a summer visit from Rome, I overheard Nonno Francesco tell a friend how proud he felt of his sons: they had built the most useful things for Delianuova, a sewage system and a school. When I reported this back to my parents, my father remarked:

'I wish we had also built a football stadium.'

'What nonsense I have to hear! A hospital, that's what you should have built!', was Mamma's comment.

In Delianuova there was one form of children's entertainment disapproved of by the adults. It was linked to death and funeral rites. When someone died the corpse was kept at home for a day or two. A couple of rooms were set aside in the house for the flow of visitors. The men were in separate quarters from the women, who sat vigil in the room with the deceased.

As an outward sign of their grief some female relatives let their hair down loose on their shoulders. Some of these women chanted laments celebrating the life of the dear ones and how much they would be missed. There were also specialist women wailers who were occasionally engaged by the family. The children found the chanting and the stories about the deceased interesting and often amusing. Angela was always on the alert for news of deaths and of the location of the vigil. Gathering a few trusted friends, she would set off towards the house of bereavement and position herself to best advantage for looking and listening. She and her friends would mimic the wailers in the days to come until the next funeral. Mamma forbade her these expeditions. Angela carried on.

Mamma Giulia' cooking: aubergines for balls, fritters and cutlets

Melanzane ripiene was – and still is – the special Ferragosto dish in Delianuova. However, aubergines play a big part in everyday Calabrian cooking and particularly in my mother's. From May to September there were not many days in which a *melanzane* dish was not presented to us. In our affluent years there would also be peppers or courgettes, green salad, tomatoes, thin beans often made into a salad with fresh tomatoes. In winter we would have preserved aubergines.

Before we move on to specific dishes let us clarify a couple of details regarding selection and preparation of aubergines. The best are those firm to the touch and smallish – by which I do not mean the baby ones but the smallest among the fully grown ones. The stalk should be removed. As for the skin, some dishes are better without it such as *polpette*/medallions; some best with a partial removal. In other dishes such as *melanzane ripiene* the skin is essential.

The next big unresolved issue is the bitterish taste of aubergines: should it be removed or not? My mother maintained that it should be removed. I know of very good cooks who do not bother. How is it to be removed? In dishes that require boiling, even if only for a couple of minutes, the removal is automatic. In all the others the procedure my mother followed was this: slice/cut the aubergines as required and place them on a colander in layers. Sprinkle a generous amount of salt on each layer. Let them stand for at least a couple of hours during which they will shed a darkish liquid and their bitterness with it. You can then remove this liquid by taking handfuls of aubergines and squeezing them with your hands. I have to say that the aubergines that I buy in London supermarkets are not very bitter. So, on the whole, I think that this laborious procedure may be dispensed with.

Polpette di melanzane

When making *melanzane ripiene*, as I described at the end of Chapter 9, Mamma always made sure to have extra meat and aubergine mixture over and above what she needed for the boats. Meatballs can be made with meat only as the basic ingredient (see Chapter 6) or with a mixture of meat and aubergine. You need one aubergine per about 200gm of minced meat. Peel the aubergine and cut into small pieces of about 1cm cubed. Boil them for about ten minutes, drain them and let them cool before mixing the resulting pulp with the meat. Add one egg, chopped parsley, garlic, salt and breadcrumbs. Extra water may be necessary depending on how watery the aubergine pulp is. No milk should be used. I now regularly prepare a largish amount of *polpette* mixture – whether with aubergines or not – and I freeze part of it in appropriate portions for a meal. When it is thawed, I mix it again and often need to add a little extra breadcrumbs for consistency.

Meat and aubergine medallions/fritters

The meat and aubergine mixture can also be used to make medallions, a dish welcomed by all the children. I occasionally prepare them for my grandchildren. The mixture is shaped into thin circles of about 4cm in diameter. Sprinkling the two sides of the medallions with flour helps to keep their shape and makes for easier frying. Once fried, the medallions should be treated to the usual fat absorption process with kitchen paper. They are delicious with aperitifs. Sometimes I shape the mixture into larger medallions and grill them. They make tender hamburgers.

Vegetarian balls and medallions/fritters

The boiled aubergine pulp can also be used on its own, without the minced meat, to make vegetarian balls or medallions. Use three to four aubergines peeled, cut in small pieces and boiled. Squeeze out much of the liquid and let the pulp cool. Then mix with one egg, breadcrumbs, some grated parmesan and chopped parsley. You can also add some finely chopped garlic. Season with salt and pepper. The mixture must be soft but not runny. Add breadcrumbs if it is too runny or water if it is too hard. Take a small amount into your hand and shape as a small medallion. Sprinkle with flour on both sides and fry them, turning over once. The fritters - whether of meat and aubergine or fully vegetarian - make a lovely accompaniment to aperitifs.

The aubergine pulp can be shaped into little balls and baked in tomato sauce. Use sauce both underneath and on top of the balls. They are lovely served with rice and another simple vegetable such as peas, beans or carrots.

Cotolette di melanzane o zucchine

This is an ideal dish for vegetarians or just vegetable lovers like my family. It is also a good way of serving vegetables as a main course. Thin slices of aubergines and/or courgettes can be used to make cutlets not dissimilar to meat cutlets. There are two versions of this recipe. They are both suitable for vegetarians and both taste delicious. I slice both vegetables lengthwise. I do not peel the vegetables except for the two outer slices of *melanzane*.

In the first version I dip the slices of aubergine or courgette in beaten and salted egg and then coat both sides with breadcrumbs. Fry at a high temperature in about ½cm of oil. When removing them from the frying pan place the slices onto kitchen paper. This is the same method used to prepare meat cutlets in many Italian families.

In the second version I lightly coat the slices with white flour, dip them into the beaten egg and fry.

11

Men

... the
Bitter air of exile
Is like a poisoned wine.
Anna Akhmatova

Building was one of the many trades and crafts among the Delianuova men. There developed also a strong tradition of stone carving
done with the local serpentine or *pietra verde* – green stone. The
works of past artists can still be seen in local public fountains and
in several portals gracing the entrances to old landowners' homes.
Mimmo Papalia, a gifted, local sculptor, is continuing the tradition
in the twenty-first century. Carvings were also made from wood,
particularly olive. This was a special skill of the Caminitis, my
Uncle Corrado's family. They and other skilled artisans also made
individually commissioned pieces of furniture which were often
carved. Other craftsmen included tailors and shoemakers as well
as a guitar maker and a basket weaver.

In my childhood the community also had its own *banditore* –
town crier – who was sent all over the town to shout the latest
news: an edict from the mayor or the arrival of fresh fish in the
market or – more commonly – the disconnection of water supplies.
One man occasionally entrusted with this job was an unfortunate
choice. Feeble-minded and lame, his speech was also highly defec-
tive. Deciphering what he was trying to convey was quite a challenge. At times we children were sent to approach him and extract

the message face to face.

Shopkeepers tended to sell manufactured goods from groceries to textiles and haberdasheries. In these shops women could spend hours discussing patterns and colours of material or the shape and size of buttons. These were goods brought in from Reggio and Messina. As regards footwear, the very poor people of Delianuova – usually the peasants and olive gatherers – did not wear shoes. They went barefoot or wore clogs made within their own families or bought from local artisans. For quite a few years after World War II shoes were made by bespoke shoemakers. Then gradually ready-made ones started coming in and the shoemakers switched to repair jobs only.

There were also a few jobs for educated people such as lawyers, doctors, pharmacists and, of course, school teachers. Whether the artisans, shopkeepers and professionals did well or not depended on olives. The economy was largely based on agriculture and specifically on olive crops and the production of olive oil. People used to talk of lean years when the olive produce was poor. A poor olive crop meant a lean year for everybody. The ownership of the land was very concentrated and some landowners commanded huge estates. Many families had smallish plots just large enough to produce the oil they needed for family consumption.

But even in good years the olive and oil industry could not generate enough jobs and earnings for families. The olive economy was run largely through the hard work of women, on which more in the next chapter. For the majority of men there were very few opportunities for local employment. They had to emigrate. The USA, Australia, Canada and South America were early destinations. After the war years there was a surge of emigration to Germany, France and Belgium and, later, northern Italy. Families were torn apart. A few days before the dreaded departure the emigrating man and his family usually gave a farewell party. Scenes of great anguish would follow his departure. Was one's husband, son, brother going to the land of *sperduti* – those who forget – usually the USA or northern Europe, or to the land of *perduti* – those who are completely lost to the family back home – usually Australia or Argentina. Occasionally we would hear that some émigré, often a woman, was feeling unwell and very low in the new country.

'*L'aria non n'ci coli*' (the air does not agree with her) was the usual pronouncement of friends and relatives. Whether the air was congenial or not, it was very difficult to return to Delianuova. The marriage arrangements as well as the financial difficulties of paying for travelling back home made a return almost impossible. They became *perduti* whether by choice or necessity.

Emigration also created a few business opportunities for people with a little education. Zio Domenico - Micu - Scutellà and a few other enterprising men took advantage of the growing need for intermediary services in the emigration process. He set up an agency assisting the would-be emigrants to get through the paperwork and the bureaucracy needed to pass medical checks, get visas and book passages on ships. He arranged for groups of people from Delianuova and surrounding areas to travel together. They could then give each other support during the journey and on arrival.

Education was a scarce commodity in the Delianuova of my childhood. My various uncles and aunts never had the opportunity of being educated further than the five years of primary school, except for the two youngest Iettos. Only one of them, Raffaele, availed himself of the opportunity offered to him. He attended middle and secondary school in Reggio Calabria. The youngest, Francesco, was not academically minded. Angela and I were the first university graduates on either side of the family, though many of the younger cousins followed in our footsteps.

For the older Ietto brothers the beginnings were very hard. Before they acquired their first car well after the war, they had to struggle with poor or non-existent transport connections when work took them to distant places. At times they got a lift in a cart or lorry or used the postal bus for part of the journey. Occasionally my father would get up at four in the morning to walk through bad roads and reach the place of work by seven. The same road would be walked back in the evening. Sometimes he found local accommodation for the whole week. When still a bachelor, at weekends - which extended from Saturday evenings to Sunday evenings - Pietro often joined his friends in serenading girls. Someone played a guitar while they all sang love songs walking along the streets of Delianuova and stopping outside the houses of sweethearts. Papà was known to lean against a wall and doze off in the upright position while his friends carried on singing.

Whenever an opportunity for better education presented itself, the older Ietto brothers jumped at it. In their teens my father and his second brother Gianni attended a course in drawing, painting and sculpting run by a Calabrese artist, Maestro Moscatello. So did my maternal uncle Rocco Scutellà. The training in *belle arti* turned out to be very useful to these three young men but for different reasons. During the war my father and his brother managed to avoid the front line by claiming special skills at drawing. They were allowed to do most of their service as draughtsmen at the Ministry of War in Rome. They never expressed embarrassment at their lack of involvement in active service. Like many Italians, they were not enthusiastic about fighting Mussolini's wars.

As for Zio Rocco, he used the acquired skills for drawing patterns on his cakes. I would watch him from a corner of his workshop drawing beautiful shapes. He used piping bags made of calico and with a metal nozzle at the end. The bags were filled with bright, coloured, soft mixtures. He would squeeze a thin line and direct it on to the cake to draw flowers, leaves, trees, angels or huts or an abstract pattern at the edge. The expression on his face was always serene when engaged in this particular task, not agitated and frowning as when he was baking and working next to his scorching oven. I would look at the movement of his hands in expectation of bright colours and enchanting shapes.

Opportunities for improvements in education were often offered by the Church. One of the middle Ietto uncles – Zio Mimmo – talked to me about it in later years:

'Grazia, when I was a teenager things seemed fixed, as if life would go on forever in the same way and with the same people in charge. Yet some people did think that change would come. Even men from the Church. A young priest had come to visit our Delianuova parish and he gave talks to boys in their teens. He lent us books and told us to be prepared for change. He talked in a very cautious way as if he were afraid to say what he wanted to say. But

7. Papà Pietro in 1950

he made clear that things would not continue as they had and that
we should expect change. It made an impression on me and only
during the war did I understand what he meant.'

As regards household chores, men did next to nothing. They did
not look after the children: a woman's job. Neither did they cook,
clean, wash up, iron or mend. They did some shopping because the
middling class of women were not supposed to go out to the shops.
In particular, the buying of meat from the butcher was considered
a man's job. The butcher's shop was open only on Sunday mornings. When our immediate family was not having Sunday lunch
with either the Iettos or the Scutellàs, Papà would be sent off to
buy meat with clear instructions on what to bring back. Inside and
outside the butcher shop there were long queues – or rather large
gatherings, as Calabrese people, like most Italians, are not noted
for orderly queueing. The butcher had only one butchered animal.

He would cut pieces of meat there and then and offer them for sale
one at a time. For Papà it was a matter of waiting till the butcher
offered the specific piece that my mother wanted. Unfortunately
the butcher started by getting rid of the poor cuts. The men who
were of impatient temperament settled for any piece going, just to
get away from the place. This is what my father usually did. Back
home, there followed scenes and lamentations on the part of my
mother to which my father's defence was:

'This was the only piece available and the butcher assured me
that it is excellent. In any case it all comes from the same animal
and so it will make good *bollito* or stew no matter what cut it is.'

In the end it did make a good meal, thanks to my mother's
skills.

Sunday was the day when most men were seen strolling along the
corso or chatting away in small groups in the piazza or sitting at
cafés. Good gathering points were also the barbershops, particularly on Saturdays and Sundays, and, on weekdays, the two pharma-
cies in Pedavoli and Paracorio.

Norman Douglas saw the pharmacy of Calabrian small towns
as the 'centre of the leisured class, the philosophers' rendezvous'.
He always applied to the *speziale* – the pharmacist – and his local
friends to get his information and 'feel the true pulse of the place'.

Gissing had visited Calabria some 14 years before Douglas. He
also expressed appreciation for the philosophical discussions of the
Calabrian middle classes:

> I spent an hour one evening at the principal café ... [w]atching
> and listening to the company (all men, of course, though the
> Oriental system regarding women is not so strict at Catanzaro
> as elsewhere in the South). ... Among these representative men,
> young and old, of Catanzaro, the tone of conversation was
> incomparably better than that which would rule in a cluster
> of English provincials met to enjoy their evening leisure. ...
> For instance, a young fellow in no way distinguished from his
> companions, fell to talking about a leading townsman, and
> praised him for his *ingenio simpatico*, his *bella intelligenza*, with

exclamations of approval from those who listened. No, it is
not merely the difference between homely Anglo-Saxon and
a language of classic origin; there is a radical distinction of
thought. These people have an innate respect for things of the
mind.

But not all discussions by the local Deliese élite were of a philosophical nature. Groups of men, whether of the middle or lower
classes and wherever they were congregated, could be seen talking
and stopping their chatter as soon as a young woman approached.
Men's eyes became fixed on her body. They would follow it along
the corso. The chatter would soon resume, often on a new topic
of conversation supplied by the passer by. Comments on her
physical attributes and her morals might be made but not before
making sure that none of her menfolk were around. Embarrassed
women lowered their heads and averted their looks as soon as they
approached these groups of men. Middle-class men could also
continue their idle, philosophical or political discussions at a newly
established *circolo* – club – while playing billiards, drinking and
amusing themselves.

The staring at women by men did not disappear with my childhood. The contemporary travel writer Karen Haid spent a few years
in various towns of Calabria towards the beginning of the twenty-
first century. She came from the USA rather than from northern
Europe, as did the traditional seventeenth-, nineteenth- and early
twentieth-century travellers, and found it disturbing to be stared at.
She was referred to as *a Mericana Mericana*, meaning a real American, not one of Italian origin.

Looking back, I agree with Gissing that Calabrians have respect,
indeed admiration, for things of the mind. I can also detect other
general characteristics among the Calabrese men of my childhood.
Quick to take offence, they were also generous towards family
and friends. Pride was the most notable characteristic. François
Lenormant seemed to agree with this. He also found the taciturn
Calabrians very dignified, honest and loyal. It seemed to pass on
from generation to generation. Several northern travel writers of

the past noted how waiters and guides eschewed gratuities. They seemed very pleased to receive just a verbal appreciation of their services. Though there was – both in their times and in my childhood – dire poverty, begging in the streets was almost unknown. Reading what foreign writers felt about the Calabresi's pride and generosity brings to mind a particular episode in my childhood. There had been a fire which almost destroyed the house of a poor but not desperate family – people with pride in their status and position. But these were times when the only insurance and welfare available was the goodwill of your community. A few weeks later, on a Sunday morning when all the men were out in the corso, my mother and other local ladies went around armed with a lined basket each. They daringly approached the men one by one or in groups and asked for small contributions to relieve the distress of a family hit by misfortune. They gave generously. No one asked who the family was.

In spite of so many uncles around me, my childhood familiarity with men was far less than with women. This had partly to do with gender segregation. My brother developed a stronger bond with his uncles. They would take him around the building sites and discuss with him building problems. This gradually gave him a strong interest in as well as the neccssary skills for taking over and developing the business in later life.

This type of intercourse with the family men was denied to us girls and instead we tended to bond with women. It was women we saw every day: men were often away, sometimes for long periods. The war took most of them away for years.

Mamma Giulia's cooking: what about potatoes?

Potatoes were not a great staple in our family. Calabrese families used to bake their potatoes in the cinders of their brazier. They then cut them, added salt and olive oil and ate them on their own or with the addition of other vegetables such as beans. Mamma rarely baked potatoes. But occasionally on a winter's night she stewed them as follows.

Stufatino di patate

Cut the peeled potatoes into small chunks, about 2cm cubed, and wash them. Lightly fry a finely chopped onion and add some tomatoes peeled and cut small. Mamma would use the preserved variety in winter and the fresh, ripe and succulent ones in summer. In London I now use tinned tomatoes. Add the potatoes to this mixture. Cover the pan and let them simmer till tender, adding a small amount of water from time to time. The *stufatino di patate* was occasionally served on its own as a vegetable. It was a favourite with the whole family.

Mamma often turned this dish into a full meal with the addition to the potatoes of cold meat such as leftover *bollito*. The meat – cut into small pieces – must be added a few minutes before the potatoes are fully cooked. A full vegetarian stew can be prepared by adding broccoli or cauliflower florets and carrots to the potatoes. *Stufatino di patate* in all these three versions is one of my husband's favourite dishes.

Pasta e patate

There seems to be something excessive in putting together two starch ingredients, yet the result is a delicious winter soup. Lightly fry a chopped onion and add some tomatoes. Add also a small carrot and a piece of tender celery cut very small as well as a potato chopped up in small pieces (about 1cm cubed). For two people I use a largish potato. Add some water from time to time. Turn off your heat a couple of minutes before full cooking. Separately, cook some small-shaped pasta (for two people 50gm is enough). Before it is fully cooked, remove from the heat, pour some of the water into a bowl and keep it in reserve. Add the pasta to the potato pan together with some of the pasta water. Add extra pasta water if necessary and also some extra olive oil before serving.

Sformato di patate

Later in our family life, when we were in Rome, Mamma learned two new potato dishes: gnocchi and sformato di patate. This is a potato pie suitable for cold winter nights. She made the former dish rather rarely and this may be the reason why I never learned to do it. Both dishes require the mashing of boiled potatoes. She always added some olive oil and a small amount of milk to the mashed potatoes.

Mix most of the mashed potatoes with small pieces of lean ham and hard-boiled eggs chopped up. Place the mixture in an oven dish lined with grease-proof paper and cover with the remaining mashed potatoes, those to which no ham or egg has been added. Sprinkle the top with breadcrumbs. Bake at 200 degrees for some 20 minutes.

Mamma did not have grease-proof paper. But this was not such a problem. The hardest part of this dish, oddly enough, was the mashing up of the potatoes. Mamma – like other Italian women of her generation – had a complicated and highly inefficient gadget for the mashing operation. Its main part consisted of a metal cylinder of about 10cm diameter covered at the base and open at the top. It was full of small holes throughout its base and circular walls. Attached to it were two handles of which one was fixed. The other was movable and had a round flat disk attached to it. The mashing process consisted of the following. She put two or three pieces of boiled potato into the cylinder, lowering the movable handle to make sure the flat disk attached to it entered the cylinder and was placed on top of the boiled potatoes. Then she pressed the two handles together to mash and squeeze out tiny lines of potatoes from the holes in the cylinder. Complicated? Inefficient? Yes. And tedious, hard work too for Mamma, though we children enjoyed seeing the tiny, wiggly bits of potato emerging from the contraption. Many years later Mamma was delighted when I brought her a simple, standard potato masher from London.

12

Women and their lives

e mi chiamavano intorno
le soavi donne d'un tempo,
e la madre, fatta nuova dagli anni,
la dolce mano scegliendo delle rose
con le piu' bianche mi cingeva il capo.

around me called
the soft women of ago,
and, by years renewed, my mother
her gentle hand choosing roses,
with the whitest ones she garlanded my head.
Salvatore Quasimodo

In Delianuova the lives of men were hard. The lives of women were no better. Those from very poor families scraped a living working as gatherers of olives. They moved with their children to the countryside from October to December, living in shacks and huts. This was the period when the number of schoolchildren in classrooms drastically declined. The women spent the day in the groves, bent towards the ground, picking olives often under lashes of wind and rain. The modest ones among them wore an apron at their back. At a time when the wearing of trousers for women was unthinkable, this trick helped to hide olive gatherers' upper legs and underwear from men's eyes. This may have protected their moral health but there was no protection for their physical health. The hard work and unsanitary conditions shortened their lives and those of their children.

Women were considered good at carrying weights. Gissing recalls an amusing incident upon his arrival in Calabria by boat from Naples. On landing at Paola on the Tyrrhenian coast he was approached by half a dozen men scrambling for the privilege of carrying his luggage. The winner approached him and, with a satisfied smile, presented a woman who had been waiting nearby: '*Mia sposa, signore!*' (My bride, sir!). The woman seized the heavy luggage, flung it on her head and carried it up the hill.

Women worked on building sites alongside masons; they moved bricks and stones, carrying them on their heads. In his *Gente in Aspromonte* the Calabrese writer Corrado Alvaro discusses women carrying stones in the 1920s. The hard work and graceful bearing of these women in the 1930s is described by Andrea Giovene in his *L'Autobiografia di Giuliano di Sansevero*.

Some women worked in other people's homes as full-time servants or doing occasional jobs for well-to-do families. These were the women from families in desperate straits. Often they were widows or wives of the emigrants who had not yet been able to send back money or who had abandoned them. There were also a few women working as school teachers or dressmakers, embroiderers and weavers. Augusto Placanica traced a vibrant silk industry to sixteenth-century Calabria. It was wiped out by competition from the north, particularly after Italian unity. Some remnants of it may have lingered on. My cousin Daniela told me that one of her older women relatives used to put silkworms in her brassière to keep them warm and productive.

In the house next to my grandparents there lived a family of some three men and four women, the children of one of my grandfather's cousins. Their parents were dead and they were very poor. The girls tried to earn a little as weavers using a hand and foot loom. To meet tight deadlines on commission they often worked at the loom alternately to keep it going all day long. The loom was in the ground-floor room, next to my grandparents' front door. The weavers were extremely nice to me and Angela and I loved to sit in a corner and watch them working. I longed to be hands on and was fascinated by the loom. Multicoloured threads were set vertically and horizontally in long straight lines. The weaver's hands passed the shuttle spools between two sets of threads meeting at a small angle on the horizontal part of the loom. The movement of the feet caused the threads to move up and down in a colourful, rhythmic dance, gradually producing patterns on the developing material.

'Grazietta, what are you thinking? What do you want?' says Anna.

She knew what I wanted. Before I replied, she would lift me up on her knee and help me to thread the spool.

But commissions became more and more sparse and the finished work was not well remunerated. Eventually the girls emigrated to the south of France, where they set up a successful flower-growing business and married. Their brothers had already left for France or Belgium. Their old house was one of the two bought up by my uncles to enlarge the family home.

The lot of women who did not have to work for a living – including those around me – was also extremely hard. Not until the late 1940s was piped water available. Women fetched water from the street fountains, of which there were and still are many. Move forward 70 years. When in my London supermarket I see women pushing trolleys containing large numbers of plastic water bottles, I feel a sense of irony. I cannot help going back to a time when carrying water home was a necessity forced on women by the lack of basic public amenities.

Washing of small items of clothing was done at home or, secretly, at the local public fountain. The town council forbade washing at the fountains. The *guardia municipale* – town warden – was charged with making sure the rule was observed. The penalty was a large fine that people could hardly afford. Women used to post their children to look out for the *guardia* and give them warning. Neighbours also kept watch for each other. The problems came either when the *guardia* arrived from a side street or when children became bored and started playing with their friends and forgot the task in hand.

At this particular time, Mamma Giulia had a toddler and a

baby and was still living at Zia Domenica's house. One morning while washing my nappies she was caught by the *guardia*. He levied a fine and refused to listen to her pleas. She never forgave him.

'You know, Grazia, he was married to a nice woman; the daughter of my parents' next-door neighbours. We were friends. How could she marry such an unpleasant man? My Uncle Angelo had been a *guardia* for many years before he retired. He never treated people like that.'

On another morning, in winter, she got up very early to avoid being caught. The chill in the air and the freezing water gave her shivers. By the evening she had a high temperature. Pleurisy developed. In these pre-antibiotic times, it took her several months to recover. The event gave her a terrible fright. She often talked about it and blamed it for the tuberculosis she developed when we moved to Rome.

Large items of laundry had to be done by the small river just outside the town. On a summer day the sheets and bedspreads could be seen drying on large rocks or on tree branches. Poorer women took on these heavy items of washing for a fee. The water flowing down from the mountains was nice to drink but quite cold for laundering even in summer. Soap was home-made. This I found one of the most baffling operations. Throughout the year Mamma collected any remaining scraps of soap. She also collected in jars the leftovers of used oil, largely from frying. Here comes the baffling thing: how can dirty oil be used to make soap which will then be used for cleaning? Yet it was. Everything was put in a cauldron and a chemical was added. We children were told that it was a dangerous chemical not to be touched. The mixture was boiled for the right length of time. When cooled down, it left a solid mass to be cut into bars. Timing was of the essence to avoid ending up with a sloppy mess or a hard rock.

Bread was made by the women every fortnight. Large ovens with open fires were run privately and families could use them for a fee. Facilities for mixing were also provided. Large quantities of dough were mixed early in the morning or late at night. The timetable had to be observed strictly, as the ovens were scheduled for use by different families each day. The dough was shaped into large round loaves of approximately 30cm diameter, slid into the oven with a long wooden palette and retrieved after the baking. The bread tasted delicious. Darkish and with a strong texture, when spread with olive oil and accompanied by olives, it provided many a Calabrese family with a meal. Moreover the strong texture of the bread made it storable for a couple of weeks. Darker colour and even stronger texture were characteristics of the so-called *pane jermanu*, German bread made of rye. We rarely had this in our family.

On one occasion the fortnightly bake became a problem for my mother's family. On a summer evening grandmother Grazia made her bread. As the story was related to me years later, she absently mindedly put in the correct amount of salt twice. There was no question of discarding such a large amount of bread: it had to be eaten. The family pretended that the extra salt was hardly noticeable. Nonna Grazia knew better. She spent the fortnight crying every time her family sat down to a meal.

Another big job was the preservation of food for the winter months. Cheese, for example, was salted. None of the various branches of my extended family kept a pig but they would buy one before Christmas and have it slaughtered. The whole family then sat around the kitchen table and prepared the meat. The mood was very jolly in anticipation of the *frittole* feast in the evening. These are the fat and hard parts of the pig such as trotters that would be boiled and served first hot to a feasting family and their friends, and later cold. The fat was preserved separately, as was the jelly, a green trembling mass. I felt a sense of magic seeing how the white and pink flesh of pork was turned into a green jelly. We children called it *trema trema*, wobble wobble. It provided nourishing spreads for the winter months. Most meat was preserved by converting it into sausages and salami. This process required great skills to prevent air bubbles forming and developing mould. This was a skill that the Scutellàs had and the Iettos seemed to lack, according to my mother.

Mamma never made jams and marmalade. Some fresh fruit was available all year round. There was, nonetheless, much activity in the preservation of vegetables and fruits: beans – largely butter beans – aubergines, tomatoes, figs. They were usually sun-dried by spreading them in large, rectangular, shallow baskets placed on terraces and roofs. Olives were preserved in large jars filled with brine.

The preservation of fresh tomatoes and the making of passata for the winter required considerable skill. It is a hard and labour-intensive process done in the summer months. Bottles were used as containers and they had to be thoroughly washed first. The best tomatoes were selected, washed and cut into long thin slices to be put into the bottles. We were enlisted for this operation, as small fingers could more easily push down the tomato segments. The tips of our fingers became wrinkled but it was fun. The bottles were then sealed and placed in a large purpose-built cauldron for boiling on an open-air fire. Relatives, friends and neighbours cooperated in a jolly, festive atmosphere.

Among women's lighter jobs were the more ordinary tasks of cleaning the house, cooking, washing, ironing, mending and sewing clothes for children. In the lean years, particularly during the war, every scrap of material was used for new clothes. Mamma often dyed old, white material to make it into a more attractive base for her daughters' dresses. On one occasion her dying skills failed her. She used material from old pillow cases with a white-on-white raised pattern similar to the Paisley design. She wanted to dye it red. It came out dark purple.

'Oh dear me! It is all wrong. How can I dress my two little girls in funereal purple? What can I do to save my material?'

She came up with a solution: she brightened up the dresses with a white embroidered collar and some little white trimmings on the bodice and hem. I felt very pleased with the final outcome. I liked the hidden pattern in the material and the fact that it was visible only close up.

'Can you see anything special in my new dress, Maria?'

'No. Nothing. What is it, Grazietta?'

'Come close and see. Closer still.'

'Yes, there is something; a pattern; like a leaf. What is it?'

There was one specific area in which Deliese women had an edge over women in the urban environments of later decades. They could always rely on a relative, friend or neighbour for help with heavy chores. The same friendly women were occasionally enlisted to buy one or two hours of peace.

Often enough I had heard my friends mention how they had been sent to fetch *u mpedicu russu ca manica d'ossu*.

'It is such a wonderful experience. The *mpedicu* I was offered was a vivid red – *russu* – and with such a delicate bone handle – *manica d'ossu*.'

I had never seen one and felt quite envious. Then one day my mother tells me:

'Grazietta, go to Zia Maria and ask her to give you her *mpedicu russu ca manica d'ossu*.'

I jump to it. So Zia Maria has it and here is my chance to see and touch one. When I deliver my message to Zia Maria, her two eldest daughters are working at their embroidery. They smile. She remains calm and serene as usual.

'Grazietta, what have you been doing lately? Tell us about your friends and what your brother and sister are up to. We'd like to hear it.'

I oblige but after a while my thoughts go back to the purpose of my visit.

'Zia Maria, my mother wants *u mpedicu russu ca manica d'ossu*.'

'Yes, I know, Grazietta. But be patient. Talk to Aida and Elena. Ask them to sing songs for you.'

Time passes very pleasantly but I return to my mission. Eventually Zia Maria says she will go upstairs and look for *u mpedicu*. She comes back after a long time and pronounces:

'Grazietta, I am very sorry. I looked everywhere and could not find it. I have not seen it for a long time. I must have mislaid it.'

It took me years to realize that this was merely a ruse by adults to gain an hour or two of peace and quiet. Now, *mpedicu* is quite an unusual word even in dialect. This is the only language in which I have ever heard it and indeed only in relation to children. It is difficult to translate into Italian, let alone English. Roughly it means the object or process by which someone is made to 'hang/linger around', 'keep busy'.

Women's lives were very restricted. As in many pre-industrial societies, women's mobility was seen as a threat. Young women of good families did not go out on their own except to church. They were often restricted even in their shopping expeditions. They did not travel on trains or coaches by themselves for many years after the war. George Gissing during his 1897 travels by the Ionian Sea noticed how women above the poorest class were not seen in the streets. He remarks that, in Cosenza, 'Only on Sunday did I see a few of them about the street; they walked to and from Mass, with eyes on the ground, and all the better-dressed of them wore black.'

When I was in my mid-20s during a study year in the USA I visited my Uncle Pino in Canada. Like many emigrants his view of Italy had not caught up with the pace of change in Italian society brought about by the *miracolo economico*. He was delighted to see me but said that he was surprised that my father would allow me to go to America on my own. It had never crossed my father's mind to query my travelling plans especially if they were for study reasons.

I often wonder how my Aunt Velia coped with these mobility restrictions. She was from Pesaro in the Marche region where Zio Gianni met her during World War II. They had a quiet wedding in Rome and then settled in Delianuova. We had a party for the newly-weds. Special food was prepared and close relatives and friends were invited to meet the bride and feast. Everybody worried about whether we would be able to understand her Italian and whether we were refined enough for a woman from the north. We children expected her to be in full wedding dress. She was not. She wore a white dress with some light-blue trimmings. Tall, blonde, blue-eyed, she seemed to come from a different planet. She befriended us children almost immediately and we were proud to be able to understand her Italian. My little cousin Lilli – her mother's nickname for Mariangela – came not long after to delight us.

Velia was accustomed to moving around Pesaro on her own, whether on foot or on a bike. Both were unheard of in Delianuova. She longed to have a go on a bike and one day she seized her chance. My youngest Ietto uncle, Ciccio, was in his early teens. He had several friends, one of whom owned a bike. Often they all had a go on it, riding along the Paracorio side of the corso, in the final stretches leading outside the town. She made a deal with her brother-in-law and went for a walk accompanied by us, her nieces, along the corso. She met up with the boys, mounted the bike and off she went. The rumour spread faster than her pedalling and soon scores of children were running after her, shouting:

'*Na fimmina 'nda bicicletta, na fimmina 'nda bicicletta*' (a woman on the bike, a woman on the bike).

She never tried riding again. Looking back, her loss does not seem as serious as that of Barbara Kovalenka in Chekhov's short story *Man in a Case*. Barbara was denied a much desired marriage proposal by riding a bike. Chekhov thus describes the horror of seeing a woman on a bike:

> Belikov changed colour from green to white and he looked stunned. He stopped, looked at me and asked, 'Would you mind telling me what is going on? Are my eyes deceiving me? Do you think it is proper for high school teachers, for *ladies*, to ride bicycles?'

Mamma Giulia's cooking: quick, inexpensive, healthy *pasta asciutta*

Sauces for *pasta asciutta* are numerous and very versatile. They can be based on vegetables, fish, meat or a mixture. They can be very, very cheap or more expensive. The ones I list in this chapter will hardly make a dent in your income. They all have in common the potential for making a meal that is delicious, healthy, inexpensive and easy to prepare. You need approximately 75–100gm of pasta per person for a main meal. All the dishes in this section are best with the long type of pasta such as linguine or spaghetti. Neither Mamma nor I ever used *bucatini*, that funny long pasta with a hole in the middle. It is difficult to cook and even more difficult to eat as it is too thick to roll up easily on your fork. If you would like to try it, I suggest wearing a bib when eating!

Spaghetti/linguine all'aglio, olio e peperoncino

This is a classic quick dish for when there is nothing else in the house. It is, traditionally, a main resource for young people starving in the early hours of the morning after a night out and still wanting to spend time together.

Lightly fry some cut-up garlic in a small amount of oil and add some red chilli cut into very small pieces. Meanwhile boil the pasta and drain. Pour the drained spaghetti into the frying pan and cook for a few seconds while stirring. Before serving, sprinkle some breadcrumbs to absorb any excess oil.

Spaghetti/linguine al prezzemolo

In a small amount of oil fry some chopped garlic. Meanwhile wash a large amount of parsley (almost one fistful per person) and chop it up. Boil your spaghetti or linguine. Drain it and toss into the frying pan, adding the parsley and some extra oil. Mix together, add black pepper and you have a delicious first course.

Spaghetti/linguine alle acciughe

Most people have tins of anchovies in their cupboard. They are good in salads but they are also extremely good for a special pasta sauce. You need one 50gm tin of anchovies for 150–200gm of pasta. Discard the oil in the tin and place the anchovies on a flat dish. Separate them and cut into small pieces. Place them in a largish frying pan with a small amount of olive oil and a couple of spoonfuls of hot water from your boiling pasta. Cook gently till the anchovies melt, no longer. Do not add salt to the cooking pasta: the anchovy sauce will have enough. Drain the pasta and pour into the frying pan with the anchovies. Add olive oil and stir. Before serving, sprinkle with breadcrumbs to absorb the oil. Use crumbs made from real bread only and without any additions. This ingredient is widely available in Italy, though many Italian delicatessens in London now sell it.

13

Far bella figura

'... for my pies are fit to show with the best o' my neighbours'; and
the linen's so in order,
as if I was to die tomorrow I shouldn't be ashamed.'
George Eliot

Zia Velia's social and open-air life was very restricted but her
husband did his best to compensate. As soon as economic conditions improved, a lovely house was built for his growing family.
When the firm acquired its first car – a Balilla – he started taking
her to Reggio where he often went on business. Velia took these
opportunities to enjoy a meal out. She also liked shopping in the
regional capital.

'The best fashion accessories are to be found at la Signora
Versace.'

Lower-middle-class families were always keen to *far bella figura*.
After the war the Iettos began, gradually, to position themselves
a few steps higher in the *bella figura* ladder. Economic conditions
were improving fast. The brothers' skills were in high demand as
postwar reconstruction got under way. One step was to be climbed
with the acquisition of two fur coats: one for Velia and one for
Giulia, the only two daughters-in-law at the time. The two coats
came with problems. They had been given by a Reggio furrier
in part exchange or as a thank you present from a very satisfied
customer – the brothers had done some building work for him.
The two sisters-in-law and their husbands went to Reggio to select

their fur coats. Mamma chose black and Velia chose brown. For some reason the coats were not brought back home immediately but came with Gianni and his wife on their next trip.

The first big problem arose when my mother saw her coat. She insisted that it was not the one she had chosen but a much inferior one. To make things worse the brown one for Velia seemed to be of a higher quality. Mamma smelt a rat and began complaining to my father about bad behaviour on the part of his brother and wife. Papà tried to calm her down:

'Fur coats are nonsense; they all look the same to me except for the colour. You wanted black and black you got. I do not want to hear any more fuss.'

In the end a family quarrel was averted. But worse was to come for me. I intensely disliked the fur coat. I thought Mamma looked awful in that ragged garment that seemed no better than a sheep-skin. The coat was too short, just above her knees, not wide enough to button up and with high and rigid shoulder pads. I never saw my mother look more ridiculous but I kept my views to myself. Merci-fully, she only wore it a few times and did not take it to Rome when we moved there.

But two wears were enough for me to commit an offence against my mother. We children, or at least Angela and I, understood the whole saga about the coats and how they came to be in the posses-sion of our families. However, Mamma wanted her friends and the rest of the town to think that the coats had been paid for in cash and not as part exchange or a present. Payment in hard cash looked more impressive. We promised to keep mum. Unfortunately, after her first Sunday outing in the fur coat I met up with my friend Maria for afternoon play.

'Your mum went to Mass in a fur coat today. My mother and aunt think it is great. They do not have a fur coat.'

I do not want her and her family to feel inferior to us.

'Maria. It is a secret. Promise not to tell anyone? If you promise I will tell it to you only.'

'I promise, Grazietta. See, I kiss my crossed fingers in front of you.'

'The fur coat was not bought. My parents do not have that

much money. It was given to my father by a shopkeeper in Reggio. Do not tell anyone.'

A few days later I overheard Mamma saying to a relative how pleased she was with her coat. After all her friend Teresina – Maria's mother – was always bragging about how she got fashionable clothes in Messina. I left the room, my cheeks in flame. I never discovered whether Maria was better than me at keeping secrets.

Looking back I can see that there were deeper reasons for resentment within the Ietto family than the quality of a fur coat. My mother had brought a dowry – the only Ietto bride to do so. Following tradition, the dowry was delivered from Nonno Nino to Nonno Ciccio. It was invested in the building business, I expect with my parents' agreement. Yet the earnings from the firm were never used to improve my parents' situation. When in Delianuova, we always lived in rented accommodation. Nonno and his favourite son Gianni – the holders of the purse – never made funds available to buy a house for Pietro and his family. My father's old, childhood feelings of rejection must have been enhanced by this unfairness. Mamma was resentful and pushed Pietro to demand fair treatment. He could not. He was afraid of further alienating his family. He had always been very attached to his parents and brothers and would often relate with pride and gratitude any small signs of affection he had received from them. Relations were always very warm and affectionate towards us children.

Keeping up one's status in the community was a must in Delianuova. Social snobbery was rampant. Only the very underprivileged and perhaps the very few rich landowners were above such worries. All those in an intermediate social position, like my extended family, were keen not to debase it and indeed to improve it. Having tidy, clean and well-furnished houses was one of the signs of belonging to the respectable section of the community.

Most houses did not have gardens. Many had small courtyards at the back or side where chickens were often kept. Houses of my relations and friends did not usually have armchairs. Most people just sat in upright dining chairs. The dining room was the place where you received guests, sitting around the table where food and drinks were laid. My parents had lovely furniture in their bedroom and dining rooms. My mother's eldest brother, Raffaele, had made two complete sets. The bedroom set included a cupboard with large mirror, a chest of drawers and two little bedside cabinets all with attractive carvings. The latter three pieces had marble tops of a pinkish colour with white and wine-red streaks. The dining room, in art deco style, had a square extendable table and a sideboard with raised lateral cabinets on top as well as matching chairs. I liked the light, warm-coloured wood and used to trace the smooth contours of the carvings with my finger. My parents did not take the dining room set with them when we moved to Rome and it became lost to the family. Might they have sold it to pay for the move?

Women were pawns in the status game. Suitability of partners on social grounds was considered essential. Brides were expected to bring a dowry, which passed to the husband or his family. Parents usually let it be known what dowry could be expected for their daughters. Negotiations might take place between the fathers of the couple whose marriage was being discussed. What women thought of the dowry system can be gleaned from this popular song:

Invece di un marito	Instead of a husband
Mi compro un bel maiale	I buy myself a handsome pig
Me lo ammazzo per Natale	I slaughter it for Christmas
Me lo ammazzo per Natale	I slaughter it for Christmas

Brides also brought a *corredo* or wedding trousseau. Young women were often seen sitting outside their homes sewing and embroidering their own wedding trousseau of sheets, table cloths, bathroom towels and bedspreads for the future marital home. Bed linen was usually embroidered white on white but table linen and towels could be colourful. Future brides would engage in long discussions with friends and relations on the choice of patterns and colours. As the work was done before marriage or even engagement, the initials embroidered on the linen were of the girl before she married. Angela and I still have some which belonged to my mother and bear her initials: SG. There were strict rules as to how many pieces were required and what type of linen was to be used to make a reasonable, good or very good trousseau. Its size and quality became a matter of family pride and status. The trousseau would be displayed to family and friends when they paid their first visit to the new bride.

Mothers started preparing their daughters' marriage trousseau from very early on. Mamma began to buy fine linens for Angela and me from when we were 14 years old or so. She bought superb items for both of us and chose them herself, usually without any input from us: it was what *she* liked. We were provided with enough to be able to pass on quite a few items to our own children. One problem with this system is, of course, that the items were bought without any knowledge of what the future household to which they were destined would be like. Mamma provided for all circumstances: I have round table cloths as well as square, small rectangular and large rectangular ones.

Weddings were occasions to display one's wealth to guests, whose number could run into the hundreds. Likewise at funerals, families displayed wealth and status as well as their emotions. After the war, at funerals of well-to-do families, one would see large numbers of wreaths. Several priests officiated. The band played sombre music. A photographer might record the procession. Food also played a part in the display of status by friends of the bereaved. It was the custom for friends and neighbours to take food to the mourning families for the first week after a death. In periods of scarcity and restraint, the amount of food was adequate and very welcome. When the local community became increasingly affluent those bereaved families with many friends had a problem on their hands. All the friends would compete to provide the best quantity and quality of food. It was not unusual to have two or three sets of friends providing for the same meal, each with large amounts of food, including cakes. The competing groups eyed each other with some hostility and the members of the bereaved family felt pressurized into accepting and welcoming all the offerings. On top of their bereavement, they often ended up with indigestion.

Clothes and external appearance were essential elements in maintaining one's status. We were told in no uncertain terms that we were the type of people who wore shoes, not the barefoot type or clog wearers. Mamma became very angry if any of us went out shoeless even for a short time. There were strict sartorial codes and the choice of clothes was a matter of great discussion. I particularly liked the process which led to my mother's acquisition of a new dress. The material was bought from one of her friends, my friend Maria's aunt, who had a shop selling textiles and fashion accessories.

'Giulia, I really recommend this piece to you. It is the very best in fashion. Not just Reggio fashion; it is Messina fashion.'

I often accompanied Mamma to the dressmaker. She patronized three and chose between them according to the occasion. One, a distant relative, was a genteel woman from a landowning family living in a large house. She started providing for a family of five girls when her husband died, by which time their land had also gone. The other was a disabled woman – *a zoppa*, the lame one – who could hardly stand, let alone walk. She cut the material with the aid of a large wooden board placed on her lap. It was known to be hit and miss whether the cutting came out right or not. The third one was a younger woman setting up in the fashion business just before we moved to Rome. She was the one my mother entrusted with preparing our frocks before we moved to the capital and in preparation for our entry into Roman society. Mamma looked at fashion magazines and would engage in long discussions with the seamstress.

'Giulia, the magazines you are looking at are the very latest in fashion. It is for you to decide what you want. Do you want a square neck line or V-shaped or round or boat shaped? Do you want a straight skirt or with some gathering or pleats? I would not do heavy gathering or too many pleats. They would make you look fat. Long sleeves are better for you as your arms are short and plump.'

'What about pockets? Should I have them? They are useful.'

'Pockets? Oh no Giulia! Pockets make you look fat. If you really insist we can have vertical slit pockets. But remember, you should not use them to keep your handkerchief or keys in.'

Discussions could go on for hours, with every woman in the workshop joining in to give her view. The cutting of material and how it related to the finished dress intrigued me. The shape for breasts came out not from a wider cut of the material around the chest, as it seemed natural to me, but from restricting the portion of material underneath it with darts. The top of a sleeve was cut with a roundness that seemed to bear little relationship to the cut to which it would eventually be attached in the shoulder part of the dress. It all seemed mysterious and yet, in the end, it all fitted together. Three trying-on sessions were considered necessary to arrive at the finished product. More than three was a sign that something was wrong and the dressmaker was not that good after all. I attended all of them with Mamma. I particularly liked it when the seamstress checked the evenness of the hem. She set up on the floor a wooden ruler fixed vertically to a small base; it helped to mark the desired distance between floor and the bottom of the dress. Mamma would turn around very slowly while the seamstress, kneeling next to the ruler, stuck pins on the hem. She kept some pins between her lips and took them out as necessary. At the end of the process I would offer to gather from the floor any fallen pins with her horseshoe metal tool. I loved to see the pins jump on to the magnet. At the time, I was planning to become a seamstress in my adult life. Move forward over 70 years. The fashion for uneven, up-and-down skirt hems may have made redundant the process I so much enjoyed.

There was considerable discussion among women about fashion, patterns and colours. The fuss about colours seemed particularly strange because the most common colour seen on women was black. In my childhood, there were strict rules about observing mourning dress for dead relatives and sometimes for friends: so many years for a brother, so many for a parent or a child. Men wore black ties and, for a while, large, black armbands. Women dressed totally in black. Indeed for the first few weeks or months – according to the closeness and age of the deceased – they would also cover their heads with black kerchiefs. Unmarried women were allowed to wear black for shorter periods. Married women hardly ever came out of mourning once they got into it because there was always

8. Mamma Giulia in 1971

someone dying in the family.

The convention was not to wear black for the death of a child up to one year of age – there were too many of them. Yet the anguish of the parents was not diminished by a less funereal dress code. Following a sympathy visit, Mamma recounted how sad a friend was at the recent loss of her baby. Crying inconsolably, Assunta opened up to her friend:

'Inside me I feel so black that I do not see why I should not be allowed to wear black on the outside. Who are these people who dictate what I should or should not wear? How dare they criticize me if I want to wear black? What do they know of the anguish of losing my sweet baby?'

She later managed to have two surviving children.

Mamma followed the accepted code for women in a good social position: cleanliness, tidiness and sober elegance. She was pretty. Not very tall, she had blue eyes and fair hair which turned auburn in later years. She never wore make-up but was very keen on perfume and, like my father, took great care of her hair. When in Delianuova, she let it grow very long, almost reaching her bottom.

She braided it into two thick plaits worn as a coronet around her head or looped up on her nape. Later, when in Rome, she had it cut a little shorter and wore it in a chignon. As a young woman Angela became skilled at make-up and hair dos and often helped Mamma with brushing and setting her hair in a beautifully finished chignon. When the family became affluent in Rome, Mamma never missed the weekly appointment with her favourite hairdresser. As she grew older she had it dyed an auburn colour and set in a chignon to the very end of her life.

Mamma Giulia's cooking: delicious, non-meat dressing for *pasta asciutta*

Pasta with asparagus

Mamma never cooked asparagus. This is one dish that I developed in London where asparagus is plentiful and excellent. I chop up an onion very finely and let it soften in a small amount of oil at low temperature. Add asparagus tips cut in pieces of about 2cm. Cook for about ten minutes adding small amounts of water now and then. I like to use hot water from the cooking pasta. When this is ready I add a few drops of lemon juice. Separately, I cook pasta, usually the smallish variety such as *penne* or shells. After you drain the pasta dress it with the asparagus and onion mixture. You will need a little extra oil.

Spaghetti/linguine con zucchine

A courgette sauce can be made by lightly frying the courgettes cut into small pieces. Add their flowers if you are lucky enough to get them. Discard the excess oil and toss the drained pasta in the frying pan with the courgettes. My sister has developed a good variant on this condiment. She lightly purees the courgettes with the addition of grated parmesan cheese. I tried her version. It is easy to prepare and very tasty. You can use either spaghetti/linguine or *pasta corta* for either versions of this dish.

Spaghetti al pomodoro fresco

This is a summer dish when the tomatoes are fresh and succulent. Peal your tomatoes and discard the seeds. Cut the flesh into small pieces and place in a bowl. Eliminate excess liquid. Add plenty of olive oil and some black olives. Use with-stone olives and remove the stones yourself. Leave the mixture to marinate for about half an hour. Cook your pasta and before draining add a good amount of cold water to cool it down. This dish should be eaten tepid. Toss the pasta into the bowl with your condiments and serve, topping it with torn basil leaves. This dish is also delicious and more nourishing if you add to the tomatoes – with or without olives – fresh mozzarella cheese cut into small pieces.

Spaghetti al tonno

This was one of my father's favourites and it is now one of my husband's. Mamma made a simple tomato sauce using lightly fried garlic rather than onions. Before the sauce is fully cooked add a tin of chopped-up tuna and let it simmer for a couple of minutes. Mamma never used the oil from the tin and neither do I.

Spaghetti alle vongole

This is one of my very favourite dishes. It is on offer in most Roman restaurants and I have been able to make it in my London home in the last few years, as *vongole* – clams – in their shells are now sold by London fishmongers. I allow 300–350gm of clams in their shells for 160–200gm of linguine. One hour before dinner I place the *vongole* in a colander over a pan or bowl. I let a tiny flow of water run over them. This operation eliminates any remaining sand. Cook your linguine without the addition of salt; there is plenty in the *vongole*. Meanwhile lightly fry cut-up garlic in a very small amount of oil. Toss the *vongole* in the frying pan and raise the temperature. Cover the frying pan with a lid to retain as much as possible of the liquid. Within a couple of minutes the *vongole* open up. Lower the temperature and let them cook for another 3–4 minutes. They are now ready to receive the cooked and drained linguine. Let the pasta and *vongole* finish cooking together in the frying pan for a few seconds while mixing them. Discard any *vongole* that do not open: they are not good for consumption. Top up with extra oil, chopped fresh parsley and some black pepper. Dish out the contents of the frying pan and some fish gravy on to each plate. Supply your family/friends with bowls for the shells they are going to discard. When eating your pasta and *vongole* take the shell in one hand and with the fork in the other remove the clam. Roll your spaghetti strands – no more than a couple at a time – round your fork, pick up a clam and pop into your mouth. Delicious!

Pappardelle o tagliatelle ai funghi porcini

Mushrooms have always been a great delicacy, available free and in abundance in the woods around Delianuova. On a September morning, after the July and August heat followed by the first rains of the season, mushroom picking was the thing to do. Groups of friends and sometimes whole families did it. Adults knew which mushrooms to avoid. They were cooked fresh, fried or stewed as vegetables or made into a pasta condiment. Many families gathered enough for preservation either as dried or blanched and kept in jars filled with oil. Some enterprising families developed funghi preservation into small cottage industries. The finished products were distributed via intermediary businesses in Reggio.

I like *pasta con funghi*. The best type of pasta for this dish is egg *pappardelle o tagliatelle*, particularly the mixed green and yellow. I use dried ceps and follow the instructions for soaking, allowing 10gm of dry ceps per person. I discard the liquid in which they have soaked and rinse them at the end. Fry a chopped onion and add the ceps cut into small pieces. Simmer, adding a little water from time to time. I use boiling water from the cooking pasta. After you boil and drain your pasta, add it to the frying pan with ceps and stir for a minute or so. Before serving add chopped parsley. My friend Giovanna adds some peas to the ceps to soften the taste. Many cooks – particularly in the north of Italy – add some cream to the frying pan with pasta and ceps. I prefer the simpler, less rich version.

14

The local health service

They brought someone in from the railway, a switchman. I got him
on the table to operate, and damned if he didn't have to die on me
under chloroform. ... I sat down and closed my eyes like this. And
I thought of the men and women who will be alive a hundred or
couple of hundred years after we have gone, those we're preparing
the way for. Will they have a good word to say for us?

Anton Chekhov

My mother's other source of pride and distinction was cleanliness. She was scrupulous about food, bodies and the home. Our
undergarments had to be as tidy and clean as our external clothing.
Her love of cleanliness turned out to be particularly useful in her
healthcare role – she had a reputation for skill in nursing. People
were sent to her by the doctor or, most often, came on their own
initiative to consult her in preference to the doctor. She dressed
wounds, gave injections and offered advice on diet and hygiene. It
was all done free of charge, though we often received presents of
fresh eggs, ricotta, vegetables or – more rarely – a chicken in return.
On one occasion she assisted the doctor in removing a large cyst
from the shoulder of one of our neighbours.

Our local general practitioner was a nice, friendly person who
knew the community very well. His manners and care made up for
his limited skills and the scarcity of drugs. When he judged that
injections were necessary he would often involve my mother. She
had a couple of syringes of different sizes and a few needles, one

of which was reserved for the family. In practice that meant herself and me, as none of the other three would allow her needles to go anywhere near them. The same glass syringes were used over and over again for different people and medicines, and were sterilized by boiling before and after the treatment. She had a little oval pan made of aluminium, inside which there was a flat, perforated and removable part. Its tiny feet allowed it to sit on the bottom of the pan without touching it. In shape and concept the whole apparatus resembled a modern fish steamer on a much smaller scale. The various dissembled parts of the syringe, including the dreaded needle, were placed on the perforated part like fish on a steamer. Water was put in the pan and allowed to boil for a few minutes. She took this equipment with her when the family moved to Rome.

Her love of cleanliness met with cultural and social obstacles. She used to rant against the behaviour of some older women. As they moved towards middle and old age, peasant women often wore traditional costumes which were made of a shirt and a couple of long, large skirts, one on top of the other. Occasionally one of the old women would stop in the middle of the street, spread her legs apart and piss. My mother got very annoyed when one of them relieved herself next to our front door.

One day Mamma had a visit from a distant relative of my father. Suddenly, my brother was brought in by his friends, howling with pain. He had fallen and badly hurt his arm. Catuzza was keen to help:

'Urine, urine. You want to put urine in the wound. It is salty and has healing powers. I can provide it for you immediately if you give me a bowl.'

'Thank you, Catuzza, it is very kind of you, but Franco is distressed and I must calm him down before I attend to his arm. He may calm down more easily if he and I go next door by ourselves.'

Catuzza took the hint and left. Mamma took white, soft bandages from her large supply and proceeded to clean the wound with pre-boiled water.

We three children were at the receiving end of her attention to hygiene on another matter. Both she and we dreaded lice, of which there were many around. Now and then she urged us not to play with such and such children because their mothers never washed them. Segregation was not enforced and children mixed freely with each other. Lice did jump from head to head. Three little heads were often sprayed with DDT. We survived it as we did the purges she gave us twice a year. The change of season in spring and autumn brought a change of food regime, as the type of vegetables available changed. Mamma greeted each new season by the cleansing of our innards. The evidence that purges worked was seen by Mamma in the fact that, following their ministration, we ate with renewed enthusiasm.

Mamma had great faith in intervention to prevent or cure illnesses. She did not seem to believe in the body's natural healing powers.

'But how can she recover from her fever unless something is done?'

The something to be done ranged from having special food to taking medicines, be they injections or tablets, to calling in the sorcerers. My body was the site of most of her interventions.

While I dreaded injections, there was a different type of intervention that I positively looked forward to when I was ill. As well as calling in doctors and administering medicines, Mamma also sent for the healers. They claimed both diagnostic and therapeutic expertise. Her Aunt Marianna and her sister-in-law Vittoria could both perform the appropriate ceremony, called *passare* (going over).

Zia Marianna, who was always keen to oblige, was given a pasta bowl half filled with cold water and an oil dispenser. She put a few drops of oil into the water and with a serious and concentrated expression placed herself at my bedside near my head. She slowly moved down, holding the bowl a metre or so above my bed. While moving several times around the perimeter of the bed, she whispered a recitation. My eyes were fixed on her lips and the bowl. Finally her lips and feet stopped moving. She looked with great intensity at the liquid in the bowl. She would then give her diagnosis.

'Giulia, it is as I thought. The evil eye again. Somebody has given Grazietta a malign spell. We are surrounded by evil and envious women. They wish ill to our little girl because she is so clever and good. But we shall make her better.'

Time to dispel the effects of the evil eye. Zia Marianna placed herself at the foot of the bed. She looked intensely at the water and oil mixture and then at me. More whispering of recitations. Within a few minutes she would relax and look at me with her usual kind smile. She then happily announced that I would improve within a few days. I did. For Mamma this was further evidence that there were horrible people around, envious of my academic and embroidery abilities.

These episodes generated friction between my parents. Mamma accused Papà of boasting too much about my attainments. This, she said, attracted malign attention. His view was different:

'You should not allow all this nonsense to be performed on Grazietta. If Zia Marianna wants to come and visit, fine. But no *passare* for my daughter. As for my talking to friends, I shall go on saying what I want about my little one. After all it is only the truth.'

Papà was, of course, right about the *passare* ceremony if not the boasting. However, he neglected an important point. I very much liked the whole process and it is possible that the positive impact on my mental state may have aided the natural healing powers of my body.

My Aunt Vittoria - instead of Marianna, Mamma's aunt - performed the *passare* from time to time. She was closer to us children in age. Very nice and friendly, she was always available to tell us a story. Over and over again I asked her to teach me the magic words.

'Grazietta, I promise I will to do it for you, but we must wait. I cannot pass on the healing wisdom to you till you are a full adult, over 18 years of age. It must be done by the two of us being together and on our own at midnight of a New Year's Eve.'

Unhappily, by the time I was over 18 we were in different towns and my mind was on different matters. She died without passing the secret on to me. I carried with me my health problems to the next stage of our family life in Rome. Mamma took her excellent culinary skills, her syringes and her love of the family.

After a bout of illness longer than usual in spite of several *passare* sessions, I am allowed out and we have Sunday lunch at the Iettos. On this early summer evening the five of us leave the Ietto grandparents' house and walk downhill along the stretch of corso that takes us home past the Scutellàs' café and house. Angela and Franco are teasing and daring each other. Our five figures project long shadows. I suddenly realize that if I walk a little ahead of the rest, my shadow will project further. I feel a sense of elation at the thought that I, little Grazietta, have suddenly and by magic become taller than my brother and sister and even my parents. I go to bed in a happy state wondering whether 'Ntoni and his goats will bring us milk the next morning and whether my favourite small goat will look at me or just wander off.

Mamma Giulia's cooking: food for ailing bodies

Stracciatella

This soup is delicious, very nourishing, easy to prepare and has the added bonus of being very pleasing to the eye. All you need is meat broth, eggs and grated parmesan. I like to use good-quality broth made with a mixture of shin of beef, a skinned chicken piece, a couple of carrots and celery stems, an onion, parsley and some ripe tomatoes. The process is described in Chapter 6. I usually make a large amount of broth and freeze it in portions.

For the actual *stracciatella* – literally, small rugs – I allow half an egg per person. Mamma allowed one egg. Remove the meat and vegetables from the broth and strain it. Separately beat the eggs and then add to them a good amount of grated parmesan while you keep your broth boiling. Add the egg and cheese mixture to the broth and whisk with a fork. Florets of egg will form on the surface in about one minute. Your *stracciatella* is ready. Serve hot. The meat and vegetables make an excellent main course when hot. Green sauce – as described in Chapter 17 – is a very good accompaniment. You may have leftover meat and cooked vegetables which

can be used for a main meal the next day. Cut them up and add to
stewed potatoes (see Chapter 11).

Accarezza stomaco: dishes to caress your stomach

Pastina all'olio

What do you give your child or husband when they have an upset
stomach or have just come back from a difficult day and want something light, quick and easy to cook? *Pastina all'olio.*

In a relatively small pan with boiling water cook some *pastina*:
very small shapes such as *conchigliette* or cut-out *capelli d'angelo.*
Drain part of the water leaving a small amount of liquid. Add some
oil and eat hot. If you are just tired and worn out you can add
grated parmesan but do not if you are suffering from an upset stomach.

Verdura, patate e zucchine

What do you give your family the day after a big binge? The following was a typical meal after the Christmas, Easter or Ferragosto
festivities. In fact, my mother would buy at the same time the huge
quantities of food for the festivities and the lean food for after-
wards. It is a typical Calabrian thick soup, one of the mainstays
during the war years.

You need a good amount of *bietola* (chard and/or similar large
greens such as pak choi), one or two courgettes cut into thick slices,
one or two large potatoes peeled and cut into about 2-3cm cubes.

Wash the *bietola* and cut into smallish pieces. Put in a large pan
with some water. After a little while - the timing depends on what
type of green is used and how long it might take to cook - add the
potatoes and, later, the courgettes. If necessary, add extra water.
When all the vegetables are cooked, add salt and a very generous amount of oil. The finished product should have quite a bit
of greenish liquid. The actual amount of liquid you allow partly
depends on taste. When ready, let it rest for 15-20 minutes before
serving.

It will help to repair the damage of overeating in previous days.
Mamma made it also for anybody complaining of constipation.

PART II
MOVING NORTH. STAYING SOUTH

15

North we go!

... questo nostro paese, così piccolo, un pugno di case!
Non posso mai liberarmene, non posso dimenticarlo!
Se anche vado a finire in Canadà, me lo tiro dietro!

This village of ours, so small a fistful of houses!
I can never free myself from it, I cannot forget it!
Even if I end up in Canada, I shall take it with me!
Natalia Ginzburg

On a scorching July day in 1950 we board a train at Gioia Tauro on the Tyrrhenian coast to take us to Rome. At first the wooden seats in the third-class compartment are cool. The train is not too crowded till it reaches Naples. We three love the novelty. Franco makes friends with children in other compartments and organizes games of hide and seek and cowboys and indians. Angela and I look out of the window and comment on what we see. For the two of us, this is not the first train journey nor the first visit to Rome.

We had been taken by my parents in 1946 for a short visit to Zio Raffaele – Mamma's eldest brother – and his wife Zia Pina. This first visit stuck in my mind. We had our photos taken by a professional photographer. Mamma brought with her our best outfits – a blue skirt with double-breasted jacket and white shirt for Angela and a flowery dress with a ruche around the breast and shoulders for me. I am furious. They are dressing Angela as an adult and me as a baby. They do Angela's hair in ringlets but I am

9. Grazia in Rome: those two bows and that flowery dress!

told that my hair is too thin for ringlets. To make things worse, Mamma insists on two bows for my hair and a single, large bow for Angela. I am inconsolable. Zia Pina and Mamma do their best to coax me:

'Grazietta, you look lovely! Your style of dress is the real fashion for older children in Rome. I can assure you,' says Pina.

'Calm down; we shall take with us a replacement dress for you. We shall ask the photographer for his views. If he thinks the other dress is better for the photo, we shall replace the one you are wearing,' says Giulia.

I calm down and cheer up when I see the reassuring photographer and his equipment. In the photos a sweet smile illuminates a babyish face. The flowery dress and the two bows look just right.

At the Termini station in Rome we were met by the kind and affectionate Zio Raffaele. We all travelled to his flat in the Monteverde area of Rome. There were several attractive, three-

10. Angela dressed more as an adult and with one bow only!

storey buildings in their road, all run down or damaged by the war. The open countryside started at the end of the road. In later years it became fully built up for miles and is now a fashionable middle-class area of Rome.

It is still a mystery to me how we managed to fit in. By then they had their first child, my cousin Aurelio. The flat had two rooms: a bedroom and a dining room. Zia Pina was particularly proud of the latter. It had just been completed by the skilled hands of her husband. The corridor was a good size and so was the kitchen where we took turns for our meals. I remember mattresses on every bit of floor space. Pina and Raffaele had a stock of extra bedding from the war years. Many a stranded friend or relation, whether close or distant, knocked at their door seeking refuge or a meal, though food was more difficult to offer than shelter. Romans who had no money or connections to the black market found life even more difficult than the Deliesi. People would talk about the generosity of

Pina and Raffaele, as well as other Calabrese people in Rome, for years to come. My father and his brother Gianni, who were working at the Ministry of War in Rome, found a welcome home in that Monteverde flat. Papà used to tell us how on one occasion he had had a close encounter with death on his way to the flat. He was wearing civilian clothes and carrying a small case when he heard shooting by German soldiers. He ducked down and used the case to protect his head. When able to start his walk again, he realized that the case had a hole in it.

Angela and I slept in the big bed with Mamma and Zia Pina:

'Grazietta, you have a lot more strength at night than during the day. You kick really hard at your mother and me.'

Within a couple of days the van with our possessions arrived from Delianuova and we moved into the flat my father had rented for us – a two-bedroom flat in a cul-de-sac in the Tuscolano area of Rome not far from the Basilica of San Giovanni. Trains became part of our life. Their puffing lulled us to sleep and their whistling became a reassuring sign of normality.

The kitchen was a reasonable size. A table with a marble top was accommodated within it. When we had guests the table was moved into the more spacious entrance hall. We children all slept in the same room. Angela and I shared a bed. This third-floor flat was rented from a lady who came at the end of each month to collect her rent. Elegantly dressed with hat and high-heeled shoes, she wore make-up and smoked non-stop. We saw her as a sophisticated lady, and Mamma always took special care with her clothes and ours on these days. After the landlady left, Mamma would mutter how she could well afford to be elegant on the high rent we paid her. Angela and I imitated her speech, dresses and smoking. We giggled. The whole family roared with laughter.

After a year Papà was given a salary increase and we moved to a three-bedroom flat on the top floor – the ninth – of the same building. The biggest asset of this new home was its large terrace. The lift broke down often and I struggled up slowly, stopping at each floor for a rest. The flat was rented from a middle-aged priest, *monsignore*, who also came to collect his rent once a month. Sometimes he brought us chocolates. In one of the flats there lived a not-so-young woman on her own. Mamma commented on how odd this was and how the lady looked sad and lost. She soon revised her judgement.

Like all apartment buildings at the time, ours had a concierge: a married woman from the northern part of Calabria. We became friends with her two children and Mamma with the concierge, *la portinaia*. She occasionally stopped at the conciergerie for small talk. The law required that heads of households in each flat give the *portinaia* a certificate stating the family composition and the relationship of each inhabitant to the others. The concierge was supposed to keep this documentation and its contents secret and show it only to the police on request. One day Mamma mentioned how sad it was that the lady on the seventh floor should live on her own.

'Signora Ietto, do not worry. She is not on her own all the time. Watch out for where Monsignore goes after he leaves you. I should not tell you all these secrets. But you are a Calabrese like me and I am sure you would never betray me.'

'Oh! No, of course not. You can be sure of that. But I thought he went there to collect his rent.'

'Yes, he may do. Well, cara signora Ietto, you will be surprised to learn that you and I are among the very few married women in this building. They all pretend to be great ladies but most of them live in sin.'

Further details followed in the days, weeks and months to come. Mamma gradually made friendly overtures to the other lady inhabitants, married or not – a greeting, an offer of help with carrying up shopping bags, the right remark about the ladies' children. Two little brothers on the first floor took a liking to both my mother and Franco who became skilled at entertaining them. This family had a telephone and the lady occasionally took calls for us. We had to wait for over a year to have our own line.

Mamma settled down to her routine of cleaning, shopping and cooking. The local open-air market was good, though she found it expensive compared to Delianuova. My father's salary, which seemed huge from the perspective of Delianuova, looked hardly sufficient for her family's needs. She learned to cook Roman dishes. *Pomodori col riso* became a favourite. We tasted butter for the first time. She occasionally prepared a *merenda* for us of buttered bread with small anchovy pieces on top. It was delicious and a very welcome change from bread and olive oil. She did not buy it often. Butter was costly and difficult to keep during the summer, as we had no refrigerator.

She managed to find a butcher considerably cheaper than the other local ones. The meat was tasty though a little dark and not all the cuts she wanted were available. She talked to Zia Pina about this who decided that she wanted to try this good-quality, cheaper meat. When they approached the shop Pina read the sign:

'Giulia, I know why the meat you get is so cheap. It's horse meat.'

'Really? How do you know?'

'Well, the shop sign says *Carne Equina*.'

'*Equina*? How was I to know? Why do they not just say *Carne di cavallo*? Oh! does it matter? My family seems to like it. It is cheaper and I can afford meat more often. I will carry on with it. It is good for Franco. I am worried about him. He is always unwell these days.'

We gradually absorbed Roman ways and culture. Without noticing or meaning to, we became more secular. We started celebrating birthdays as well as – and later in preference to – name-days. We enthusiastically celebrated New Year's Eve and New Year's Day. Mamma embraced with pleasure the Roman custom of eating lentils with *cotechino* (large sausage) on New Year's Eve, a custom I have taken with me to London. The legend has it that the more lentils you eat the more money you are likely to earn in the coming year. One explanation often given for this popular belief is that the round, flat shape of lentils reminds one of coins. My own take on this is that if you are poor you may want to encourage your family to fill up with lentils, thus allowing you to provide only small amounts of expensive meat or fish and thereby saving money for the New Year.

Mamma Giulia's cooking : meat dishes

Inexpensive *carne equina* may have been welcomed in those early, financially tight years. Later, when conditions improved, Mamma did cook quite a bit of top-quality meat, though vegetables were always prominent at our dinner table. I here give some of her meat recipes. They are not specifically Calabrian.

Cotolette panate (breaded cutlets)

For this dish you need very thin cutlets of chicken or beef. I usually cut my own from a chicken breast and use a meat basher to thin the cutlets. Dip each of them in beaten egg and then press it over the breadcrumbs. Use those made only from bread without additions. Fry in shallow oil – about 1cm – and place over kitchen paper to absorb the extra fat. Sprinkle with salt. Dab it with paper on the upper part. This dish can be prepared ahead of your dinner party and kept warm. It is also very good served cold. One advantage is that the meat *frutta* (is fruitful), as my mother used to say, i.e. it does not shrink when fried, thus giving good returns on your money and efforts.

Scaloppine al vino o al limone

Escalopes can be made with cuts of either chicken breast or beef. Spread some flour on a flat dish and press the cutlets on to the flour on both sides. Fry them in shallow oil, place them on kitchen paper and sprinkle with salt. Prepare some lemon juice or some wine; in either case dilute with water. Use white wine for chicken and red wine for beef. Just a couple of minutes before you want to serve, place the meat into a frying pan with no addition of oil. Heat up and then pour the mixture of either wine or lemon juice over the meat. Turn to make sure all the meat receives the juices. Sprinkle with chopped parsley and serve hot.

Stufato di pollo

Neither in Calabria nor in Rome did I ever see a chicken being roasted whole as in Britain. I learned this delicious and efficient way of cooking chicken from my mother-in-law. Apart from the dishes above, there was another very good dish my mother often prepared for us: stewed chicken.

Use largish pieces of chicken such as thighs or legs and place them in a large saucepan with some oil. I always remove the skin from the chicken pieces to avoid excessive animal fat. Let them brown on all sides at high temperature. Half-way through, add a chopped onion. When the browning is complete add some white wine and let it evaporate. Lower the temperature and simmer till fully cooked. The addition of slices of peppers enhances the flavour. I usually lightly fry them separately for a minute or two and add them to the chicken a few minutes before it is fully cooked. Serve with rice.

16

Settling down in the capital

Through food we learned that there were other people in the world.
Maya Angelou

There lived on the outskirts of Rome a distant cousin of my mother – a pious primary-school master, highly respected and trusted by both my parents. He advised them to send their children to private Catholic schools. Franco was enrolled in the one he taught at. He kept an eye on his special pupil and supported him. Franco soon learned to go to school on his own, managing a longish journey by public transport and some difficult city crossings.

Angela and I were enrolled at a nearby school for girls run by French nuns. It was a *scuola media*, for the education of children in the three years following primary school. Angela should have started *scuola media* a year earlier but this was not possible in Delianuova, where only primary education was available. Our parents were keen to get her back into academic schooling and thus Angela and I began our long period of studies and life together: eight years of school followed by four years of university, sharing textbooks, doing homework together, sitting at school desks next to each other, always in the front row because we were the smallest.

Our parents thought this arrangement would ensure mutual support and protection. In a way it did – even too much perhaps. It created a very strong lifelong bond between us, which later extended also to our families. But it was not without its problems.

From the very beginning we, unconsciously, allocated roles to ourselves: I was the academic girl and she the beauty. In fact we were not that different, either physically or intellectually. We developed the other side of ourselves after separating and starting work in different fields. Angela became a very dedicated and successful high-school teacher. She met Pasquale, a fellow schoolteacher, at her first job in Anzio.

Mamma accompanied us on our first visit to the school. She wanted us to wear our best dresses. Before moving to Rome she had new clothes made for us and we were delighted. I had an additional reason to be pleased: the new dresses were exactly the same for both of us. This made me feel more grown up, though it irritated Angela.

One of the garments made by the young dressmaker in Delianuova was a mustard-yellow dress. The finishing touches included a hand-embroidered flower pattern around the neck and near the hems. The dresses were sleeveless. This was in keeping with what Delianuova society thought to be the fashion in the capital. For our first meeting with the Mother Superior, Mamma dressed us in our best: the yellow sleeveless frocks. The Mother Superior said nothing in front of my mother and made sure we enrolled first. She later gently commented to Angela and me:

'Your mother dresses you very nicely. She is really a good mother to you. Are all your dresses without sleeves? You know, it is better for girls to be modest and not show the upper part of their arms.'

During our first year in Rome Angela and I used the American trunk for our homework. Reinforcing braces made its surface uneven, so Mamma put on top of it a large wooden board. This was a detachable part of the kitchen table: an extra piece common to all Italian kitchens and normally used for spreading the dough of home-made pasta. Doing our homework on it was uncomfortable. It was too low and there was no room to stretch our legs. They had to be extended sideways along the sides of the trunk. Now and then we spilled ink on it, so Mamma had to use the reverse side on the rare occasions when she wanted to make pasta or pizza. Franco

11. Grazia and Angela in 1949

did his homework on the kitchen table.

After about a year, Zio Raffaele made us a proper desk. Made of mahogany, with side drawers and a glass top, it was sleek and shiny. Mamma was proud:

'Now we even have a desk. Make sure you keep your books clean, tidy and without dog ears. Guido, the *portinaia*'s son will help you to cover them with strong brown paper. He is good at these jobs. Books will help you to learn and prepare for a better life. I do not want you to end up like me. Anybody can do what I do. You must learn to do more. If you study now you will have a life of your own later.'

Angela and I shared those books. We read aloud the same page at the same time, taking turns. We commented on what we understood or failed to. We worked steadily and conscientiously and did whatever was required of us. Within a few months we could easily explain to Mamma why the meat she bought was called *equina*. I enjoyed Latin with its logical structure. Learning verbs and conjugations became an amusing challenge. We learnt it in parallel with the history of the Romans. It all made sense of the language and of what we saw of ancient Rome around us.

But all was not well on the academic front. The major challenge was Italian. Following one of my essays the teacher called me and quietly asked:

'Grazia, you wrote *la guanta*; what is it?'

'What you wear on your hand on a cold winter day.'

'But it should be masculine – *il guanto* – not feminine.'

I blush.

'Yes, I see. I thought it was feminine, like in Calabrese.'

The teacher – a nice, strict, young lady just out of university – looked speechless. She asked to see my mother. She explained that we were bright, able and hard working but needed to improve our Italian. The family should speak Italian at home and not Calabrese. Easier said than done. How could we speak with Mamma and Papà in a language foreign to us all? Within a few weeks the teacher proposed a different solution:

'Angela and Grazia need a little extra support for a few weeks to improve their writing skills in Italian. Do you know any teacher who could give them extra coaching?'

'No. Could you do it? They like and trust you and so do my husband and I.'

'It is not really allowed. Can you guarantee that the nuns will not be informed?'

'Yes I can. Please help us.'

So my parents paid for extra lessons. We all kept mum. With the help of our teacher, we learned fast and improved within a few weeks. She was by far the best teacher in the school. Other subjects were often taught by unqualified nuns.

There were many diversions and amusements on offer. Zio Raffaele took us to the zoo, and, as soon as we had settled down in our new home and before the start of the school year, Zia Pina offered to take us on a visit to the basilicas. It was Jubilee year and this was the recommended way to gain indulgencies in the afterlife. We visited all four basilicas, recited prayers in each and kissed the

12. Franco in the 1950s

bronze foot of St Peter. Rome was full of pilgrims and the crowds were oppressive. I saw almost nothing of the basilicas apart from the ceilings. We came to a stall selling Catholic souvenirs. A priest next to it made the sign of the Cross over the acquired object and the customers. He recited something and I became curious to know what he said:

'Ble ... em; ble ... em.'

'What is it you say? My niece wants to know what words you recite.'

'Oh! It is for American pilgrims. I say "bless them", which means *benedetti*.'

Papà bought our first radio. Angela and I listened with enchantment to a weekly dramatization of *The Mill on the Floss*. Maggie's distressed call to her brother Tom remained with me for years. Papà and Franco followed the football games and the whole family looked forward to the cycling races. Coppi and Bartali, the two cycling heroes of postwar Italy, became heroes in our household. I always favoured Bartali, the fastest cyclist on the plains, but Angela favoured Coppi, the fastest on the hills and mountains. Our discussions on the relative merits of our sporting heroes mirrored similar discussions on our preference for the Homeric heroes to which our teacher was introducing us at school: Angela took Achilles' side and I Hector's.

We socialized. Franco made friends with boys from our building and other nearby ones. They used to call him from the street and off he went for a football match or other energetic game. Angela and I stuck together. We slowly made friends with other girls in our class and arranged Sunday afternoons together. We went to the cinema from time to time. I loved it. Films provided me with long periods of daydreaming entertainment. The two hours spent in the cinema were followed by many, many hours creating my own developments of the story line of the film. Over and over again I would refashion the plot, refining it and adding or cutting scenes. On one occasion a Western film – our favourite genre – sparked off a story that required riding out of town. In my fantasy, I saw myself galloping along Via del Tritone and doing battle in Piazza Barberini to push my way from enemy lines. These are locations in the centre of historical Rome and even in the 1950s they were packed with people and cars.

Daydreaming had been easier in Delianuova. It was always possible to find a quiet corner upstairs or in the courtyard or in the street or just sitting on the threshold of our front door. In Rome, privacy was almost impossible. Bedtime was my best chance for daydreaming and my fantasies would lull me to sleep. During the day the opportunities were more limited. Sometimes I shut myself in the bathroom in search of a few minutes of privacy to finish my story. Other members of the family often complained about the length of time I spent there.

In the first few years of our Roman period, I was not the only member of the family seeking privacy in the bathroom to indulge in childish fantasies. On one occasion Franco got into deep trouble. The family woke up to find a blocked toilet. A plumber removed the pan and discovered a pile of *giornaletti* (comics) roughly folded but otherwise more or less whole. The finger of suspicion pointed immediately to Franco. He had been forbidden to read *giornaletti* and told to concentrate on his studies. The toilet had helped him get round that unwelcome restriction.

Though cinema was a favourite entertainment for Angela and me, it became also a source of pain. It took some time for me to realize that actors shot in the film did not actually get hurt or die. I felt a terrible anguish inside me at the thought of such handsome men being prepared to die. I thought they were doing it because the film producers paid them well and their death provided for their families. But it was very hard to accept.

This sadness from those earlier years resurfaced decades later in London when my son seemed worried about scenes from television or books. I wanted to ease his pain:

'What you see on TV is not real, Marco. It's all pretend. Don't worry.'

One day this rebounded on me. We had been watching the political campaign for the general election leading to Mrs Thatcher's triumph in 1979. When the result was announced I gave vent to my strong emotions against our new leader in all the flurry of Italian speech and bodily movements. Mark, then four, reproached me:

'Don't worry, Mamma. She is not real, we only saw her on television.'

Very soon we children became discerning enough to realize that our parents were wasting their much needed money on largely inferior education. Moreover we learned how to fend for ourselves in the capital pretty quickly.

When we finished our middle school Angela and I encouraged our parents to allow us to move on to state education. We also decided to play safe and enrol in a type of school that would secure us a job at the end of it. We chose vocational training in book keeping cum accountancy (*ragioneria*). At the time a diploma in *ragioneria* did not qualify one for entrance to a university. Luckily for us, the law was changed a few years later, so when we finished our state secondary school we enrolled in a university course in economics and commerce. Together, on the same course once again.

While at high school the issue of boy–girl attainment resurfaced. I had been at the receiving end of it in the Delianuova parish church during the pre-Easter competition for the number of *Via Crucis* prayers recited. In Rome one of my Ietto uncles asked me:

'Grazia, I know that you are doing really well at school. Are you, in fact, top of your class?'

'I do not think so. There is a boy, Mario, who always seems to get marks a little higher than mine.'

'Grazia, do not worry about this. He does better because of the natural intellectual superiority of boys. If you are doing almost as well as Mario, you must be very good indeed and should be proud of it.'

I did not know what to make of this. I was both pleased and upset. In later years Mario also became an academic economist and worked at La Sapienza University in Rome. We remained the best of friends all our lives.

School performance led to another cause of bewilderment. There had been a prize-giving ceremony at which Mario and children from other classes were honoured. A week or so later I was told to go to the *preside*'s (headmaster's) office. I felt nervous. The *preside* was a figure of fear, rarely to be seen. Occasionally he would stroll along the corridor looking ahead and giving no sign of noticing any of us children. This was the first time I had entered his office of dark, heavy furniture and upholstered chairs in green leather. It was forbidding. A few more children from other classes were already there. The *preside* was standing behind his large desk and we were asked to stand in front of it. The deputy *preside* directed the proceedings. We knew him well and he knew each of us. The preside told us that due to a clerical error, we had been omitted from the official prize-giving ceremony. He gave each of us a testimonial to our achievement and added:

'I also take this opportunity to tell you that the common saying "First at school, last in life" is not true. You can do well in life. I wish you well. Congratulations to all of you.'

Decades later I learned that his brother had become a very

successful explorer. Might he have been the least successful at
school and yet the most celebrated in life?

By our second year in Rome Mamma was often poorly with coughs,
sweats and the odd fever. Eventually she saw a doctor, a young grad-
uate who had just started practising in the area. She had already
consulted him about Franco who also seemed to be often poorly
– something to do with his glands. He needed nourishing food and
medicines.

With Mamma the problem was more serious. X-rays revealed
that she had a chest infection. We were not to divulge this to
friends, teachers or neighbours. Zia Pina in fact suggested we say
that she was suffering from a nervous breakdown. It seemed a
more middle-class type of illness. It was not till years later that we
learned of her tuberculosis. She was soon unable to go out. Angela
rose to the occasion and took charge under Mamma's direction. I
helped. On the way home from school, we bought food. Mamma
got up and cooked it. Then Angela and I together washed dishes
and cleaned the flat. Angela did the heavier jobs like washing the
floors while I dusted and swept. Our homework was done after
these chores had been completed.

Mamma was luckier than her own mother who had died of
tuberculosis in 1938. In the 1950s antibiotics became available and
she recovered within a year.

Throughout our childhood, adolescence and youth there was
always the tacit assumption that Angela was not only the older and
stronger one but also the more competent in practical matters. In
comparison I was weak, young and naive.

On one occasion a neighbour in Rome sent me on a shopping
errand and I came back with the wrong items. I overheard Mamma
saying to the lady that I should not be trusted to behave sensibly in
any practical matter like that. My brother and sister were the ones
to be relied on.

Angela continued to treat me as if I were going to remain
permanently 'the little one'. When aged 13, one evening I felt a
pain around my kidneys and lower abdomen. I mentioned it to my

mother and sister. Angela's immediate reaction was:

'You can't have this sort of pain. You are just imagining it. This is grown-up pain. What I get once a month when I have my period. A little one like you cannot possibly have it.'

'What nonsense I have to listen to,' was Mamma's reaction.

Mamma suggested that I rest. During the night I started bleeding. The next day Mamma explained how to use sanitary pads. She had brought from Delianuova a large stock of white squares made of fine linen. I spent the next day at home. Angela was speechless. She then became very gentle and protective and talked to me about her own experiences of menstruation.

Mamma Giulia's cooking: when in Rome ...

Mamma picked up some delicious dishes from the Romans and she cooked them for the rest of her life. They are still very common in Roman families and restaurants.

Pomodori col riso

On summer days *pomodori col riso* (rice-stuffed tomatoes) are sold ready-made in most Roman restaurants and take-away outlets (*rosticcerie*). Many Roman families now buy them from *rosticcerie*. Mamma always made her own and so do I in London from time to time. In the 1950s she followed the custom of Roman women of preparing the tomatoes in a large oven-proof dish and sending it, via Franco or Angela, to the local bakery. In Rome not many families had an oven. We had one but Mamma reckoned it would be cheaper to have them done at the bakery. The baker put many a neighbour's dish in his oven after the bread was done. The lower temperature is ideal for cooking stuffed tomatoes. If you want to have a go at this delicious dish, here is how to set about it.

Choose very large, ripe but firm tomatoes. Remove their stalks and wash and dry them. Then slice off the top of the tomato well above the middle point to form a lid for the main body. Now use the round end of a grapefruit knife to remove the seeds from both the lid and the main part of the tomato. Discard the seeds and proceed to the second operation which should be done over a colander placed in a bowl. The reason for this is to catch the juices in the bowl while keeping the solid parts in the colander. Remove most of the flesh from the large part of the tomato, leaving it hollow. Be careful not to pierce the tomato. However, do not discard the bits of tomato flesh collected in the colander. Cut them into small pieces and place in a separate container. To the tomato juice collected in the large bowl add rice – a spoonful for each tomato, though the quantity depends on the size of the tomatoes. Let it marinate and soften while absorbing the juice for at least a couple of hours. Add to the rice the cut-out tomato flesh plus some chopped garlic, basil, salt and a generous amount of olive oil. Mix everything thoroughly. Fill each tomato with this mixture, but not excessively, to allow room for the rice to expand during the cooking process. Top each tomato with its lid. Put a small amount of olive oil on the hollow of each lid and spread with your fingers over the rest of the tomato.

Between the tomatoes add some potatoes cut in slices. Season with salt and oil. Bake in the oven at 180 degrees for about 75 minutes. The time partly depends on the size of the tomatoes. It must be long enough for the rice to cook. Let them cool down before serving.

Rice salad

Mamma usually boiled her rice either when serving with tomato sauce or for making a summer salad. The rice is then cooked just like pasta. The traditional oriental method of cooking rice via absorption of water over slow heat is one that keeps all the rice components together and is likely to be more nutritious. This is the method used in risotto dishes. They are dishes from northern Italy and Mamma never tried them, as far as I know. I do cook risotto occasionally. However, for rice salad the boiling method is better because, when boiled, the rice grains separate more easily. You need to let your rice cool down. Add a variety of ingredients, from preserved small mushrooms to tiny bits of cucumber to peas to small pieces of colourful raw peppers to chopped-up ham or hard-boiled eggs. You can use your imagination to think of ingredients that will appeal to your family. Add salt and pepper and plenty of oil. I also like to add a very small amount of lemon juice. Serve cold.

Pomodori gratinati

Ripe tomatoes can be used for another delicious dish: tomatoes au gratin. You can use tired tomatoes, those that are no longer good for fresh salads. Cut the tomatoes horizontally into half and remove the seeds and excess liquid. Place each half into a shallow oven-proof dish. Separately, prepare a mixture with the following ingredients: breadcrumbs, finely chopped parsley, garlic and plenty of olive oil. Mix thoroughly so that all the breadcrumbs are absorbed in oil. Fill the half tomatoes with the mixture and bake at 180 degrees for some 30 minutes.

Minestrone

Roman greengrocers and market stalls sell chopped-up mixed vegetables ready for this delicious soup. All you have to do is wash the vegetables, put them in a pan, add two or three cups of water and boil. The addition of a potato cut into small pieces goes very well with the other vegetables. You have to add it yourself as it is not part of the ready-made mix.

In the last few years I have been able to make this dish in London with very little effort. My supermarket sells a variety of mixed vegetables – already washed! – and all I have to do is choose the most appropriate type: a bag of greens only, a bag of mixed carrots, broccoli and others not too finely cut. I always make sure to have some courgettes and add a chopped potato. Before serving add a generous amount of olive oil. Do not use stock whether your own or in cubes. The boiled vegetables and the high-quality olive oil turn the water into an excellent natural broth for this dish.

Mamma never used ready-made stock cubes in any of her recipes. I remember she tried them a couple of times as part of experimenting in Rome. She soon decided that the final soup did not really taste of broth and was too salty. I am delighted to report that the same scepticism towards ready-made broth was later expressed to me by an excellent Scottish provider of family meals: my mother in-law Ross. She did use broth in her cooking. She made her own from bones and used it as a base for a variety of delicious soups. There is a contrast between northern and southern Europe in the matter of broths and soup. In Scotland an inexpensive broth – made of bones – is added to most types of soups. Calabrese cooks let the broth emerge from the ingredients – mainly vegetables – and from the fat and taste of olive oil. When meat broth is prepared, we use good-quality meat with the addition of a few vegetables. In this case the broth is used on its own or with the addition of pasta or for *stracciatella*.

Carciofi (artichokes)

I do not remember ever eating *carciofi* in Calabria. They are very common in Rome where a tender, soft variety is available in the spring. Mamma quickly learned two artichoke dishes. I often observed her preparing them. However, I have never taken to repeating her recipes because the artichokes I can get in London are not worth the effort. They are very large and tough. Moreover, Donald does not like artichokes. My mother tried to encourage him to eat them but with no success. He always enjoyed and appreciated all her other cooking. So, I eat them when in Rome at Easter, cooked perfectly by my sister or my Aunt Rosa.

Cooking *carciofi* involves a good deal of pre-preparation and cleaning. Even the tender Roman variety has tough outside leaves and tips. So, the first thing to do is strip the outside leaves: one or two layers. Then place the artichoke on its side and cut off the tip of the flower by about 1cm. Trim the stalk by removing a thin layer of its outside. Your *carciofi* are now clean and ready but you must do something to make them tender. Sprinkle them with lemon juice inside and outside. Mamma used to take half a lemon and rub it against all sides of the *carciofi*. Now for the cooking.

Carciofi alla Romana

Cut out the stem of each *carciofo*. Put the *carciofi* and their separate stems in a saucepan. Select one not too large: when all the *carciofi* are standing against each other, there must be no room for any of them to fall over. Inside each *carciofo* place some chopped garlic, a small amount of breadcrumbs, parsley and salt. Pour some oil inside each of them and a little bit in the pan. Add a small amount of water to the pan only. Cover and simmer slowly for about 1-1½ hours. Add a little extra water from time to time.

Carciofi fritti dorati (Fried, golden artichokes)

This is a most delicious dish as antipasto or as a side vegetable. Mamma usually had it for the family at Easter. On Easter Day we would eat it while sipping some wine and waiting for the full meal. Any left over for the next day – Pasquetta Day – are still delicious. She would warm them up for us when the Easter Monday was spent at home. When we went to the countryside for the traditional first picnic of the season, we ate them cold.

After you prepare the artichokes as above, cut out most of their stems. Slice the artichokes lengthwise: you will have four segments if the *carciofo* is small and six if large. Have some white flour on a plate. In a bowl you will have beaten an egg or two. Coat the *carciofi* slices with flour and then dip them into the beaten eggs. Fry them in about ½cm of oil at rather low temperature, turning once. As you take them out of the frying pan, place your *carciofo* segments on kitchen paper to allow the absorption of excess fat. Pat them with more kitchen paper on top. As for the stems, you do not have to waste them. You can add them to the pan with *carciofi alla Romana* or you can just boil or steam-cook them and serve with oil and lemon juice.

17

Back to Delianuova: the two Totas

Though settled in Rome, our thoughts were south. Problems within the family increased our longing for Delianuova, our old friends and our free village life. We could not wait for the end of the school year. We wanted our vacation and we wanted it in Delianuova. Our parents did their best to oblige. We were allowed to spend the two hottest months of the year in Delianuova away from them. I stayed with my Scutellà grandfather and his family while Angela and Franco stayed with the Ietto grandparents. These were the years when I developed a special relationship with two young aunts, one on the Ietto and one on the Scutellà side: my father's and my mother's sisters. They were both called Tota, short for Antonia, and were very close to each other in age. They were only nine or ten years older than me.

Tota number one

... upon St Agnes Eve,
Young virgins might have visions of delight,
And soft adorings from their loves receive
Upon the honey'd middle of the night,
If ceremonies due they did aright;
John Keats

Tota Scutellà was a little girl when her mother died, the youngest in a family of seven. Her older sisters, Maria and Giulia, were married and so she and her brother Pino were brought up by their father, their brother Rocco and his wife. Zia Angelina cared for Tota as her own child and developed a strong relationship with her. Some time during the 1950s Rocco and Angelina bought their own house in Pedavoli and moved out of the paternal home. Many years later they opened a new café on the ground floor of their new house. At first they kept the pastry workshop in the old house and went there every day to work. Tota helped them. On baking days she would get up at five o'clock to prepare the oven for her brother. Their departure left Tota feeling lonely in the evenings with just the company of her taciturn old father.

When I visited in the summer, she was very pleased to have me. She was a small, plump girl in her 20s with the emotions and aspirations of a teenager. She was very pretty and had a lovely smile that matched her sociable and happy nature. She enjoyed meeting friends and relatives to talk and gossip. She saw me as a trusted companion in whom she could confide and to whom she could express her girlish feelings. As for me, I enjoyed being with her because she treated me like a grown-up. She asked my advice on a variety of issues, something I was not used to. At home people asked my views on academic matters and nothing else.

She looked on me as a sophisticated city girl. On two occasions her trust in my skills proved misplaced. She was friendly with two young sisters who lived with their mother – the local midwife – not far away from her, across the piazza. They often boasted about their ability to appreciate opera and how wonderful it was to listen to the music and understand the drama. Tota had acquired a radio and proposed that we also listen to opera. She was sure that I, with a better understanding of the Italian language and a little more schooling than her, could decipher the words of the sopranos and tenors. We tried. I could not understand a word and blamed the dire radio reception for my failure.

The second instance arose in connection with some dress material recently bought. The pattern was in yellow, white and blue stripes of approximately 3cm each.

'Grazia, I read in a fashion magazine that unless stripes are worn in the right direction they may make the figure look more plump. But I do not remember the correct direction. Do you know anything about this? How do plump Roman women have their striped dresses sewn? With the stripes going vertically or horizontally?'

'I do not know. I have not looked carefully at striped dresses.'

During my summer vacation Tota and I often read sentimental stories in some girls' magazines she managed to get hold of. I also helped her in another way. She was frustrated at being unable to go out because it was considered indiscreet for a young woman to be seen out on her own. While I was in Delianuova, Tota could, without raising eyebrows, go out and about with me. She could also sit on her balcony with me without being reproached for exposing herself to public view.

On one occasion eyebrows were raised in spite of my chaperoning. A scandal was only just averted. Her brother Pino and his wife had sent her an elegant shirt from Canada. Tota tried it on, looking at herself in the mirror over and over again, and with a series of alternative skirts to see which produced the best effect. She asked my views on the various outfits. She eventually decided to wear it with a black skirt and to go out and be seen in it.

'Grazia, do you think this shirt is too daring and scandalous?'

'No, I don't think so. Why should it be? It has long sleeves.'

'Then I will wear it with the black skirt and black shoes. I will walk slowly along the corso. We shall do it tomorrow afternoon. Everybody will see how elegant I can be when I want to.'

Now for the scandalous shirt. It was in a pattern of white and lilac stripes each approximately 1cm wide. The white part was mildly transparent though the lilac was not. It had long sleeves and was fully closed at the neck by a collar. She wore a slip over her bra and underneath the shirt and skirt. So what could be seen – partly – were her full arms, the top parts of her chest and her shoulders.

The next day we set off slowly. She became visibly nervous as we walked along the corso towards Pedavoli. She held my hand tight and looked at me from time to time. We did not get very far. One of my cousins, Nino, was running behind us. This 13-year-old son of Zia Maria soon caught up with us:

'Tota, everybody is looking at you. They are at their balconies behind you. My mother is afraid you might create a scandal. She wants you to stop at Zio Micu's house and get a shawl to cover your shoulders.'

We stopped and remained with Zio Micu's wife for some time in the hope that women in search of gossip would get tired and move away from their observation posts. She borrowed a shawl and we returned home escorted by my cousin. She was a little disappointed but her happy nature soon prevailed:

'You see, Grazia, how backward people are in Delianuova? I'm sure that in Rome a young woman can go around dressed elegantly without raising gossip. Isn't that so? Oh, how I wish I could live in Rome!'

On one occasion her request for advice from me required research of an unusual nature. She had discussions with some of her girlfriends about which of my unmarried Ietto uncles was the most handsome. At the time, there were four young men of marriageable age. She declared herself in favour of Angelo. One of her friends, Ernestina, pooh-poohed the idea, claiming that his legs were too thin. Tota then appealed to her closest source of inside knowledge for enlightenment on the matter of legs:

'Grazia, do you think your Uncle Angelo's legs are thin?'

'I don't know. I have never seen them. He always wears long trousers.'

'Yes, but you can tell whether the legs are thin, fat or normal from the way the trouser material hangs on them. If it hangs away from the legs, they are thin.'

She asked me to find out and I promised to oblige. The next Sunday when all my uncles were at home and I was spending the day with the Iettos, I followed Angelo around to observe the fall of his trousers when he was standing, sitting or walking. He looked baffled by my behaviour.

'The legs are thin, but not too thin,' I reported to Tota.

'Right, just as I thought. I will tell Ernestina.'

One night we conducted another piece of research, this time of the metaphysical rather than empirical kind. She was a little infatuated with a man who seemed to pay some attention to her. When passing by in the piazza he looked up towards us sitting on the

13. Tota Scutellà in Delianuova

balcony. But so did many others, men and women. It was almost impossible not to look up given the prominent position at which we were seated. She wanted to find out whether he was in love with her and whether his family would approach her father with a proposal.

She had been told that you could find out your future by reciting some magic lines at midnight while looking out for special signs according to which living creature was passing by. If a dog passed, that meant something different from seeing a cat. Similarly, for a man or a woman or for old or young people. The order in which they appeared to us could also be subject to special interpretation. We waited for my grandfather to be safely snoring in his bed before emerging and placing ourselves at the window. We were both nervous and trembling at the thought that the magic might work against us and ghosts might appear. But we stuck to it and carried on with our investigations. I jumped when a large black dog started crossing the piazza. I feared it might turn into a monster or that it would be followed by ghosts who might lift us from the window. Nothing of the sort. No man, woman, monster or ghost was to be seen in Piazza Regina Elena on that warm August night. Tota interpreted the signs – or absence of them – positively.

The supposed sweetheart did not come forward. It was just as well since he had a reputation as a womanizer. Tota's father was approached with marriage proposals by several local young men and she kept refusing them. In her mid-20s she was considered old enough for her and her family to react positively to a proposal from someone from further afield. A man from Messina was looking, via an intermediary, for a nice, morally sound and homely wife. Tota was mentioned. Lured by the prospect of living in Messina, she agreed to meet the man. They liked each other and theirs turned out to be a successful marriage which produced three children. She was much loved by her husband, who cared for her during long periods of painful illness.

In later life I did not see much of Tota Scutellà, though we remained very fond of each other. She would often ask my mother about me, my family and my health. I would call her from London at Christmas or whenever I knew that she had had a recurrence of bad health. She suffered for years and yet always remained cheerful and optimistic.

Tota number two

Maggie was not conscious of unusual merit,
but it was enough that Tom called her Magsie, and was pleased with her. ... Life did change for Tom and Maggie; and yet they were not wrong in believing that the thoughts and loves of these first years would always make part of their lives.
George Eliot

Tota Ietto was the sixth in her family of nine. Pretty, with a slender figure, her pale face was lit by deep, black eyes and wavy black hair. She was and always remained very unassuming and lacking in confidence, believing that she was not pretty and was stupid and uneducated. She had primary education like most people of her generation and position and was far from stupid. My mother became part of her family by marriage when Tota was a little girl coming up to nine. Mamma did not remember ever seeing Tota at play. She was always busy helping her mother from very early on till she completely took over the care of the household while still very young.

She worked non-stop from six in the morning to late at night running the family home and providing care for her parents and brothers. Later she would do the same amount of work looking after her own home, with a demanding husband, five children and her aged mother to care for. Rarely did we see her sitting at the dining table. She ate bits of food while serving the family or later after everyone else had finished and left. She was constantly praised for her hard work and seemed to derive pleasure from it, particularly when the praise came from her brothers. She went to the 8.30 Sunday Mass, not to the later one when all the young women and men were to be seen.

One incident impressed me when I was visiting Delianuova as a young woman. By this time she and her husband had acquired a television set in the lovely house, close to her parents, that her brothers had provided for her. It had a breathtaking view over the valley. The town clock and one of the two landmark pine trees were also visible from their sitting room. We were discussing television programmes and she mentioned that she liked to watch a particular one in the evening, after dinner. But of course she would never dream of sitting down and resting while watching as she thought this would be a real waste of time. Instead she did her ironing, occasionally looking at the screen.

It never crossed Tota's mind to indulge in some amusement or leisure activity; that was not her view of life for herself. She did not disapprove of others having fun – she just never seemed to demand it for herself and no one around seemed to offer or to strongly encourage her to take any. I do not know whether she ever went to a cinema. When she and Corrado came to Rome on their honeymoon, we took them to the Opera House to see *Madame Butterfly*, the first such outing for us as well.

14. Tota Ietto

She never indulged in girly things with contemporaries nor took the initiative in looking for a husband or expressing a preference. She thought that, when the time came, her brothers would find a good man for her. A young man, a close friend of one of the brothers, declared his interest early on. When consulted, she said that she accepted their judgement. She may have been keen on him but too timid to declare it, or she may have genuinely deferred to their opinion. She married him a few years later. Prior to the wedding her sister-in-law Velia was charged with explaining the facts of life. She adored her brothers and was proud of their success. They in turn loved her dearly. She lived in their shadow and later in the shadow of her husband and children. It is an irony that these same brothers, who all married women of their choice and all loved their sister, did not try to encourage her to be more forward.

Her husband, Corrado Caminiti, was a superb wood carver, probably one of the few remaining top artisans-cum-artists in the field. Furniture making and wood carving was a traditional family activity. In 1912 his father and uncle had carved the monumental doors of the Church of the Assumption. Corrado made beautiful furniture for his own home and for those of his brothers-in-law. On these superb pieces of furniture he used his skills to reproduce works of centuries past. He had specialist magazines with illustrations of pieces from the galleries of the world. He often inserted his own variations and interpretations. He also produced original works usually done in smaller pieces and often using the local olive timber with its warm colour, changing hues and smooth surface. So pleasing to touch. A beautiful low-relief horse's head. A Madonna with child, or is it just the picture of a beautiful young mother hanging in my London home? Mirror frames and a touching depiction of Christ descending from the Cross. The latter is an altarpiece for the family tomb that his brothers-in-law built in Rome. He was very generous with his works, often donating pieces particularly to people who, he felt, understood and appreciated them. His work deserves a wider and lasting recognition and it is slowly getting it. One of his sculptures, *L'emigrante*, originally commissioned by the Calabrian community in Australia, has recently been acquired by the Museo Italiano di Melbourne. From an olive trunk emerge a woman and child looking into the far distance.

Corrado was socialist and anticlerical like other men in his family. There were a few anti-establishment men in Delianuova who were considered harmless eccentrics. After all, their ideology did not prevent them from marrying within the Church, having their children christened or having devout Catholics as their best friends or wives. Within the family Corrado was considered a rather difficult man, quick to take offence and always expecting to be served and revered by his wife. In his own way he loved her. His and his wife's lives were affected by his ambiguous feelings towards his better-off brothers-in-law. But alas!, with success and the building up of their own families, they had become more self-absorbed and less interested in Tota's well being and feelings. She was thus caught between different allegiances and loves.

15. *Horse's head in olive wood* by Corrado Caminiti, 1984

In spite of these problems I do not think that Tota was unhappy. I remember her often laughing away with her sisters-in-law or with her nieces at a silly joke while her hands were occupied with some task or another. Her expectations were so low from early on that anything made her happy. She never seemed to think that life was a search for some form of happiness. She felt fulfilled in the achievements of others. Like my mother, she was very keen for the next generation of both boys and girls to become high achievers. Her children did, and this gave her much joy. In later years I saw her and Corrado fairly regularly when I visited Rome. They were there often, visiting their children studying at Roman universities. She would bring little Calabrian treats for me to take back to London: a jar of preserved *melanzane*, or fresh oregano or chilli.

Both Totas died of cancer before they were 70 and within a year of each other.

Calabrian cooking: herbs, spices and condiments

Oregano

Tota Ietto knew that I liked a good supply of oregano. For many years she would bring a jar to Rome specifically for me to take back to London. Oregano is very abundant in the Calabrian country-side. Women used to pick it in late summer and hang it to dry in bunches. When fully dried they separated the small leaves from the branches by rubbing them between their hands. It was then stored in glass containers.

Oregano makes a lovely addition to tomato salads, pizza or aubergine dishes. I never cook oregano. It deadens the taste and is difficult to digest. It must be added raw to your food.

Garlic and onions

Mamma did not use many herbs and spices in her cooking but she used plenty of onions and garlic for her meat and fish dishes. Tropea in north-west Calabria produces excellent red, elongated onions which make a tasty addition to salads. Very poor Calabresi were known to eat bread with only oil and onions as accompaniments.

Garlic is much used in Calabrian cooking. You can cut it into small pieces or use whole cloves in stews or in frying. I find that when garlic is even slightly fried it becomes more digestible than when completely raw. Just the opposite from oregano. The taste and smell of raw garlic is far stronger than the cooked variety.

Chilli

Calabrese people, particularly men, like to enhance the flavour of their food with chilli. It goes very well with wintertime thick vegetable soups. When serving such soups Mamma always placed a whole chilli and scissors in front of my father's dish. With his left hand he would pick up the chilli by its stalk and cut tiny pieces into his soup. The usual tease came my way:

'Grazietta, now I will put a lot of this into *your* soup. It is good for you. It protects you from illness.'

'Oh no, no, Papà.'

'Oh stop teasing the children and get on with your eating,' was Mamma's reaction.

My brother has retained a taste for chilli. On his dinner table we often see a little bottle of oil containing pieces of chilli. He pours some of this hot oil into his soup or on to pasta. No need for scissors on the table.

Olives

Olives were always available on the table, to be eaten with bread while sipping wine. After years of searching, I have given up trying to find good, dressed olives in London. Donald and I now dress our own. We buy jars of black or green olives in their stones and preserved in brine. For the dressing, put some of the olives into a small colander and rinse them thoroughly to remove the brine. Then pat them dry with a clean cloth or kitchen paper. Place them in a small container and dress them with finely chopped garlic, oregano, chilli and a small quantity of top-quality olive oil. You can also add some peel from lemons or oranges. The dressed olives keep well for about four days in the fridge.

Basil and parsley

Basil plants were to be seen at all the windows and balconies of Delianuova. It is used fresh in most dishes involving tomatoes, whether fresh or cooked. The smell is released by tearing the leaves into small fragments with your hands. Parsley is used to garnish fish or pasta dishes as well as pepper dishes.

Lemon juice

Lemons are plentiful in Calabria and used widely. Tota Ietto would occasionally take a slice of lemon, sprinkle it with salt and eat with gusto. Mamma often used it in her cooking. She prepared a special condiment for grilled steak, whether beef, veal, lamb or horse.

Thin cuts of steak were grilled without any addition of fat. They were then placed on a dish with a sauce made from oregano, lemon juice, salt, a small amount of oil and often some garlic cut into small pieces. The ingredients should be well mixed together. She placed the grilled meat on the sauce and turned it once to facilitate absorption. The meat flavour is sharpened and enhanced by the lemon juice. It is a sauce I use often for grilled meat – beef or lamb – and for fish steak such as swordfish.

My own version of green sauce

I often use lemon juice and parsley to prepare my own version of green sauce. It is a very simple one. In my cooking I always aim for basic, simple flavours. I am sure that real chefs would disapprove of my naive version of this sauce but I find it easy to make and delicious with fish or cold meats. It goes very well with boiled meat from a *bollito*. I use any leftovers of this sauce to dress spaghetti.

Wash a large amount of parsley. Lightly fry some garlic cut into small pieces adding to it a few pine nuts. Place the parsley, garlic, some lemon juice and fresh olive oil in a mixer and blend. You can also add to the mix a fillet of tinned anchovies cut into small pieces. The final sauce should not be runny.

18

The *miracolo economico* reaches the family

You've never had it so good.
Harold Macmillan

I do not know when and why my parents decided to move to Rome, but among their reasons was their desire to give us children a better education. There were also reasons linked to the firm and family problems. My father had disagreements and quarrels with his brothers and father for most of his life. In the late 1940s, as the firm was expanding via regional contracts, there were discussions about tendering for contracts in the Lazio region or even nationally. My father always pushed for the wider strategy. Some of the brothers and his father thought he was naive and, if allowed to have his way, would ruin the family. His brother Gianni, the key decision-taker, was stalling and keeping his options open. He was in favour of my father testing the ground by moving to Rome. A good opportunity awaited Papà.

Galassi was the man who had helped my father and his brother Gianni to avoid the war front by securing them with office work for the War Ministry in Rome. After the war, Galassi established a building business in Rome and wanted someone competent and reliable to help him. Papà took up his offer. Galassi could not have found a more trustworthy employee, a fact which he recognized throughout his life. Years later he asked to be taken to visit my father's tomb though already old and frail.

Papà was prepared to work long hours and often went to inspect

the *cantieri* – building sites – even on Sundays. He also did some
office work in connection with ordering and keeping tabs on
materials. The pay was not very high and he could not afford a
private car to move from site to site. However, fortune assisted him.
Among the employees at the Galassi offices in Via del Corso was
Gioia Marconi, the daughter of the scientist. She owned a fairly
new Vespa. When she decided to go back to the USA, her mother's
country, she sold off her possessions. My father bought her Vespa
and used it for many years.

Office work often elicited angry remarks from Papà. It was
usually other people's office work. These were the accountants and
administrators who, he felt, did not understand anything about the
technicalities of building work. Yet they wanted to dictate to him
what should or should not be done in the *cantiere*.

'*Costruttori da scrivania* – desk builders – *sposta carte* – paper
shufflers. That is what they are. They know nothing about building
and want to tell me what materials to use and when!'

Usually the issue boiled down to the fact that administrative
procedure stood in the way of his receiving the materials he needed
on time. A fact which, in his view, caused costly delays to the works.

One of the building works had some long-term effects on our
family. The Galassi firm converted a nunnery in Via Principe
Amedeo – close to Rome's main railway station – into a hotel, the
Metropol. In exchange, the nuns were given a smaller, beautiful
villa on the Via Nomentana, a little further away and close to the
flat in Piazza Annibaliano where our family moved not long after
this. Papà took Angela and me to meet the nuns. When, later,
we moved near them they were pleased and almost adopted us.
There were, in particular two nuns who became quite attached
to us. Suor Maria della cucina often met my mother at the local
market. They exchanged recipes and complaints about the price of
food or the demands of the people they were cooking for. Meanwhile those of us at home might receive a visit from Suor Maria
l'infermiera. At the time there were two young wives of my uncles
as well as Angela and I. This second Suor Maria worked at night as
a nurse for private patients. On her way back home, and unknown

to the other nuns, she often stopped at our place. She got much needed sympathy and family warmth as well as good coffee. She felt she needed them because, though working very hard to bring an income to the nunnery, she was given no say in the running of the institution. She had grave complaints against Suor Maria della cucina. The latter provided poor food and this affected her ability to work. My mother did her best to manoeuvre herself between the complaints of the two Suor Marias. These goings on at the nunnery were discussed over lunch and used to amuse Papà:

'They are just like other women. Always bickering and moaning.'

'You are a good one to talk. Aren't you always bickering with your brothers?'

After our move to Rome, Papà kept pressing his brothers to move the business north. Eventually Gianni declared himself in favour. Galassi was reluctant to let Papà go but had no choice. He said that if, in future, for whatever reasons, my father wanted to go back to him he just had to pick up the phone and a job would be made available.

The brothers bought a spacious flat in a better part of Rome: in Piazza Annibaliano, the Trieste/Salario area. The third-floor flat had the whole piazza in front of it with a good view of the Church of St Agnese where we went for our Sunday Mass. We were delighted by the move. A couple of Ietto uncles soon moved in. They first came as bachelors and not much later their brides followed. They both had children while living with us. Mamma – by now fully recovered from her tuberculosis – took charge of this larger family.

With some difficulty Papà learned to drive a car and went the daily round of the firm's *cantieri*. He always made sure that, besides looking after the building sites for which he had full responsibility, he also kept an eye on some of his younger brothers' responsibilities. The verbal attacks against incompetent 'desk builders' and 'paper shufflers' were now directed at some of his brothers. Occasionally we heard complaints against a brother on account of technical incompetence and/or attempts to economize on the quality of the materials. This made him furious.

Other people who were often the object of his anger were incompetent directors of building works from the public institutions from which the Ietto firm was contracting. He was not really suited to dealing with this type of person and could never refrain from speaking his mind, which did not always go down well. His diplomatic brother Gianni was more skilled at dealing with bureaucrats and with the complexity of applications for commissions.

Neither could Papà refrain from telling friends and acquaintances about the success of his children or of his firm. In later life, I could almost predict and become tense with embarrassment when he was about to start talking to a visitor about the large constructions his firm had been involved in and how much money it had made. The occasion was almost always one in which his listener was someone more educated and towards whom he felt inferior.

He was extremely successful in dealing with the workforce and the construction process. The labourers loved and respected him. Years later most of them came to pay their respects at his funeral. His skills were as a project manager, dealing with the technical and organizational aspects of the works: knowing not only how a piece of work should be done but also what materials were needed, what type of labour force was required and how long it might take to complete the job. All his complaints were usually expressed during lunch. He would unburden himself and then calm down.

'Why do you have to worry the children with all this talk of *cantieri* and problems? Can't we have some rest from it?', was Mamma's occasional reaction.

'What do you mean, worry? Nobody has to worry about this. I just want to talk about it and then I forget it.'

Immediately after lunch he had a short siesta. He usually asked to be woken up after seven or eight minutes. He rose fully refreshed and calm, just on the minute without any prompting.

In spite of occasional problems and complaints, Papà was very fond of his brothers. He was at his happiest when, from time to time, on a Sunday morning he and his older brothers went on preliminary inspection visits. When invitations to bid for new building works were announced, he always insisted that there should be a preliminary inspection of the ground where the road or hospital or housing estate was to be built. He would also insist that as many brothers as possible should be involved. They could all then give their views on possible difficulties, type of equipment required and the likely cost. These visits always took place on a Sunday, the only day on which all the brothers were available. Papà was often at the receiving end of complaints – at times fully expressed to his face – from some of his sisters-in-law. They resented their husbands being taken away on a day usually dedicated to the family. By the mid-1960s there were five brothers all living in the same block of flats in Piazza Annibaliano. Some of them later moved to flats built by the firm further away from the centre.

Papà always favoured an early start. Well before the appointed time he would be on the pavement, having bought his newspaper, pacing up and down. Four or five brothers would cram into the car and off they went. Papà loved these expeditions. They gave him the opportunity for camaraderie and a few relaxed laughs as well as technical discussions with his brothers. He would come back in a happy mood, ready to talk to us about the nature of the terrain and the difficulties and opportunities of the commission.

Mamma Giulia's cooking: peperoni

Peperoni arrosto

Choose sweet peppers that are smooth on the surface and firm to the touch, without the wrinkles that indicate staleness. I always like to choose one of each available colour: yellow, red, orange, green. Place them whole, stalks and all, on a baking tray lined with aluminium foil and bake at 200 degrees. Turn them over from time to time so that all sides are exposed upward at some point. When the peel starts to wrinkle and separate, it is time to turn them over. When all sides are done they are ready. It takes around 40–50 minutes.

When out of the oven put them in a plastic bag or wrap them in aluminium foil to prevent evaporation. This preliminary operation facilitates peeling. When they have cooled down, remove the stalks

- which have probably separated already - together with the peel, seeds and stringy bits. Tear them into long pieces with your hands, not with a knife, place them in a colander and let them drain for at least a couple of hours. I usually leave them overnight. Then place them on a plate and dress them with chopped garlic, parsley, salt and oil. *Peperoni arrosto* can also be used as the sauce for a summer pasta dish.

Peperoni fritti al pomodoro

Besides being delicious, this dish has the advantage that you can use slightly older, tired peppers: those that have been left in your fridge or in the shop a little too long and cannot be roasted.

Seed the peppers and cut into strips or chunks of about 2cm square. Fry them together with onions cut into segments. Remove the peppers and onions, leaving behind as much oil as possible. Discard this used oil. In a clean frying pan put some chopped tomatoes and let them simmer for a few minutes. No extra oil is necessary. Add the pepper and onion mixture and let it cook for a couple of minutes.

This dish can be served as a vegetable or used as a condiment for a pasta or rice dish. Fried slices of peperoni can be added to stewed chicken pieces for taste and appearance. They also go very well with cold roast chicken.

19

Mamma did not do cuisine ...

The cold beef, spiced with carrots, made its appearance,
couched by the Michelangelo of our kitchen
upon enormous crystals of jelly, like transparent blocks of quartz.
'You have a chef of the first order, Madame,'
said M. de Norpois, 'and that is no small matter.'
Marcel Proust

... she did cooking for her family. Food and the provision of meals
loomed large in the family and in Delianuova society in general,
particularly in the first few years of my life, the war years, during
which food scarcity became a serious problem. Whatever ration-
ing rules may have been put in place in Italy as a whole, they were
certainly not operating in Delianuova. Provisions did not reach us,
and with the men away most families had no money to buy supplies
on the black market. Scarcity of supplies was particularly severe in
flour, bread and meat. The deprivation took its toll in centimetres:
we three children and those of our cousins who were contempora-
neous with us are the only generation who ended up shorter than
our parents. Those few born before the war and the many born
after are considerably taller. Food shortages were a cause of great
worry for my mother and she used all her resources to secure us
some food. The family owned a small chestnut grove and its fruits
became a staple in this period. During a snowy, cold winter we
seemed to eat nothing but boiled or roasted chestnuts, with the
odd mandarin and apple thrown in. She managed to grow beans

in a corner of the grove close to a rivulet. Mamma and many other women went round the countryside gathering all sorts of greens, including dandelions. By adding to them potatoes and courgettes she produced a tasty, slightly bitter, thick soup (as described in Chapter 14).

Food and cooking were equally important to Mamma when economic conditions improved and scarcity was no longer a problem. During the early years of affluence in Rome Mamma found herself providing meals for a large family. She had the resources to buy the best and she did. She enjoyed being in charge of cooking meals that were appreciated by the family. The apex period for her display of skills came some nine to 14 years after we first moved to Rome. The Ietto brothers became increasingly successful in securing contracts in the Lazio region and beyond. A few of them gradually moved to Rome first as bachelors and later as married men. At one point and for a few years, when Angela, Franco and I were teenagers, there were three families living together in two adjacent flats opened up to make one large home. An unmarried brother was also with us. It did not seem to occur to anyone at this point that the three families could and should live separately. They all moved in with us and Mamma took on a motherly role with regard to her younger sisters-in-law. They accepted it. Relationships were, on the whole, quite harmonious and affectionate.

In later years when each family had its own flat in the same building, meals together were still arranged in Rome at Christmas or at Ferragosto at the seaside home. In the mid-1960s the brothers built summer flats – all in the same building – in Tor San Lorenzo, near Rome. Many years later they also built a special room in the basement of one of their Roman apartment buildings with attached kitchen. The plan was to use it for celebrations of the extended family. But alas! Though the material conditions were favourable, the social conditions deteriorated. The brothers were gradually pulled apart from each other emotionally and socially if not workwise. My father's death in 1976 may have contributed to weakening the feeling of togetherness of the earlier years.

Mamma had an instinctive and immediate relationship with food. Put any piece of raw food in front of her and she would look at it from all sides and at once pronounce on its freshness, on the best way to cook it and on the best accompaniments. In later years when I occasionally accompanied her to the shops I could almost see her thought process when faced with raw food. Her immediate reaction was not so much how good the various groceries might be to eat but how they should be prepared and cooked. She would engage the greengrocer, butcher or fellow shoppers in a discussion of recipes, listening carefully for suggestions and ideas. She often tried them but always introduced small changes of her own.

'What do you think, would this be good grilled or fried or stewed?'

She would wait for the answer and then might say:

'I think I will stir-fry it with a bit of onion, not garlic. Garlic is no good with this.'

'Why not garlic, Mamma?'

'Oh! I don't know. I do not think garlic is suitable for —'

Her cooking always appeared to be effortless. She had a calm and natural ability to organize her time around the processing and cooking of the various types of food. She could produce a large number of dishes ready at the same time and cooked to perfection. There was no elaborate or elegant arrangement of food on the plates, yet when she came in from the kitchen with steaming food, everybody's attention turned to the colours and smell of peppers, aubergines, courgettes or meat cutlets.

We never had salt and pepper cellars on our dining table. She thought they were unnecessary:

'When my food is brought to the table, it has the right amount of salt and pepper.'

In 1968 my American friend Kathy Moretto came to visit us and brought my mother a beautiful set of salt and pepper cellars. Mamma liked them very much, but as objets d'art, not for their function. She put them in the display cabinet and left them there for years. She occasionally showed them to visitors, explaining their origin. She would talk about Grazia's nice American friend.

If salt and pepper cellars were missing from our table, wine was

certainly not. It was seen as a normal accompaniment to the meal,
like having olives or olive oil. Apart from the war years, we always
had wine on the table at lunch and dinner, both in Delianuova and
in Rome. In fact, my parents encouraged us children to start sipping
small amounts of wine from the age of ten. At first it was mixed
with water to make it more palatable. Mamma believed that it was
good for our health: to fight colds and influenzas and strengthen us
when we were studying for our exams. No one ever drank any type
of alcohol outside meal times and, as far as I know, no one in the
extended family ever had a drink problem. Neither my parents nor
other members of the extended family was a cultural connoisseur
of wines. In Delianuova Mamma's brother Micu sold wines from
large barrels and provided us with good quality ones. In Rome the
oldest of the Scutellà brothers, Zio Raffaele, knew and enjoyed his
wine. He would travel to the Roman countryside, strike up friend-
ships with small wine farmers and buy from them. For years, when
Donald and I visited Rome he would appear with wines which were
roughly bottled and clad but tasted wonderful. Raffaele's strategy
for getting good wine was not much different from the one used
by Norman Douglas some 50 years earlier during his visit to Calabria. He recommends his readers to apply to the local coachman
or priest for reliable information. 'The wine of Cirò ... is purest
nectar.'

When three families were living in a single flat with my mother
in charge, somebody was hired to do the weekly laundry. Later on
the domestic help was extended to general cleaning. We all had
our daily tasks. The two aunts, Rosa and Rosetta, looked after
their young children and attended to the cleaning and washing up.
Angela and I helped with the cleaning and ironing, at which Angela
became very expert. Our duties were flexible to allow us to attend
to our studies, in which everyone encouraged us. We had the radio
on when doing domestic chores. We sang along with the music,
sometimes from different rooms, Angela perfectly in tune, I out
of tune. Suddenly Angela would stop whatever she was doing and
burst into a rumba, twist or cha-cha-cha in the middle of the room
or corridor. She had a great sense of rhythm and enjoyed dancing.

'What nonsense I have to see,' was Mamma's usual reaction.

The key part of household activities, the provision of meals, was Mamma's responsibility. She emerged every weekday between eight and eight-thirty in the morning to go to the local open-air market. It was more or less on our doorstep. From our home in Piazza Annibaliano a long, wide road, Viale Eritrea, led on to Piazza Santa Emerenziana. Viale Eritrea had two carriageways separated by a large paved area on which the market stalls were set out. Sometimes one of us might ask:

'What will you cook for us today?'

'I don't know. How do I know till I see what is there?'

'There' meant in the market. She would decide only after a full survey of the best food on offer. She never made shopping lists. Years later when we used to go shopping together and I attempted to prepare a list, she would say:

'What is the point of all this writing? We know what we need.'

She had her couple of trusted market traders from whom she bought special items usually reserved for her. A degree of bulk catering needed for her large family made her a favourite customer and secured her the quality she wanted. I also suspect that the vendors appreciated her skills in food selection as well as her kindness. She always enquired about their and their families' health and showed an interest in their problems, on which she updated us when back home. She always bought something from these trusted suppliers, but not everything. She then walked slowly the length of the market looking on both sides to see what was on offer and compare prices and quality. This helped her to make up her mind as to what to buy and cook on that day. Only on her way back from this full inspection would she buy her provisions.

At the market she bought mainly vegetables and fruit, which she regarded as the best food to have. When her trusted trader was available she bought fish. Bread and meat were bought only from specific shopkeepers and required different expeditions. Meat became increasingly important for some of her dishes. Gone were the days of no meat due to war and postwar penury. Gone were the days of *carne equina*. Only the best cuts of veal and beef from the top local butcher would do: this was Domenico who retained a mythical status in our family for over 40 years. The cuts he had available or reserved for my mother were discussed at length with Domenico and his wife who minded the till. So were the problems of their family of five daughters, about which she knew a great deal. During the summer periods, when the family moved to the seaside at Tor San Lorenzo, she would order by telephone her weekly supply of meat from Domenico. My father, who used to commute, brought it to us.

She gradually phased out the chores of food preservation for winter which had so occupied her in the Delianuova days. The only one she continued for many years was the preservation of aubergines. She cut them into thin slices, blanched them and placed them in a colander to drain. Eventually she squeezed them with her hands to drain off as much water as possible. They were then put into cylindrical pots. On top of the aubergines and inside the pots, Mamma would place a thick, round, water-resistant wooden board. A heavy stone placed on top of the board ensured the gradual surfacing of the liquid from the aubergines. Mamma's second morning task was pouring out the excess liquid. This was the first thing she did immediately after having her home-made espresso coffee. Suddenly one morning she would show me the aubergines and say:

'What do you think, Grazia? Is it time to dress them? There has been no liquid yesterday and today. Are they dry enough?'

'Yes Mamma, I think they are ready to be dressed.'

She then took out the aubergines, cleaned and dried the pot and then put the aubergine slices back in layers. She dressed each layer with salt, garlic, chilli and oregano. When the container was almost full it was topped up with plenty of olive oil. During winter we would take out a few slices a day and eat them with whatever else she had for us. Throughout the winter she made sure that olive oil always covered the remaining aubergines to prevent mould.

For the draining process, she had brought to Rome the appropriate cylindrical terracotta pots and round wooden board which she used for many years. One of the pots now sits in the hall of my London house and makes a useful umbrella stand. As regards appropriate stones to be used as weights, she found that Rome was greatly superior to Delianuova. She soon spotted loose Roman cobblestones locally called *sanpietrini*, meaning stones used to pave the city of St Peter. They were hard, dark grey stones cut into a prismatic shape and laid with the larger and polished base at the top. She appropriated three loose stones, washed them thoroughly and used them for the next 40-plus years, storing them on her terrace. They were still there when she died, though by then she had stopped preserving aubergines.

For Mamma, eggs had to be fresh and she wanted to see the hens that had provided them. Our weekly supply came from a small farm just outside the Via Nomentana to which she and my father drove usually on Saturday afternoons or early Sunday mornings. Sunday afternoons were for getting top-quality coffee at La Tazza d'Oro in the historic centre of Rome, near the Pantheon. This was their leisure excursion. They sat and slowly sipped their coffee, then bought their weekly supply of powder and finally took a stroll around the centre of Rome. They looked in shop windows and at the strange foreigners milling around. In the evening Papà played cards with his brothers and Mamma watched television. They never went to the cinema or theatre but they both liked reading papers and magazines. Social intercourse was limited to the relatives. They never acquired new friends in Rome. They had become too affluent for their old friends and remained too shy of educated town people to embrace a new social milieu.

Mamma liked to watch television but distrusted food commercials. When we first acquired a television set in Rome in the late 1950s, one programme became a great favourite with children and adults throughout Italy: *Carosello*. It was the only one on which commercials were allowed – ten minutes of commercials interspaced with witty sketches and appealing music. Mamma liked it. However, regarding the food adverts she had strong views:

'It cannot be good food, otherwise there would be no need to advertise it. People buy good food without being pushed into it.'

When Mamma came back from the morning market expedition with her large trolley and several extra bags full of provisions, we helped her to unload. She then established herself in the kitchen for the rest of the morning till lunchtime. She often brought back little treats. If she saw something one of us was known to like, she bought it and gave it to the person with great pleasure. When Angela and I were studying hard for our autumn or winter university exams, she used to squeeze some oranges to provide extra Vitamin C. She always had something for her four little nephews, who all loved her. She had a special way with small children, whether related to her or not. She did not make a fuss over visiting friends' children, neither did she address children with questions. She smiled at them then slowly took them by the hand and led them to her kitchen where they would find something to their taste.

Lunch was the main meal of the day. It started with a dish of pasta or thick soup, such as minestrone, to be followed by meat or fish with salad and cooked vegetables: aubergines, spinach, peppers, courgettes, beans or tomatoes. Normally most of her cooking was done in the morning. In this particular period some of the uncles did not come back for lunch and therefore a full meal was provided for them in the evening. Moreover, Zio Peppino needed light food because of an ulcer contracted during his year as a prisoner of war in Germany. He was the only brother caught up in front-line fighting. When Mussolini was forced out of Rome the Germans became the enemy within. Zio Peppino was taken prisoner and just about survived by working in the kitchen.

Mamma had to cook lunch at different times for different people. In the 1950s the dearth of buildings for the growing student population in Rome meant that most schools ran two shifts. Angela and I went to school in the afternoon and she cooked an early lunch for us. Franco came back from his morning shift late to find a piping hot lunch.

Affluence or no affluence, we never had pudding on weekdays. She placed a large bowl of fruit on the table and we all helped ourselves, except Papà. She always peeled his fruit, mildly complaining about how hopeless he was but looking pleased to be in charge. In fact, she always dished out food for him and helped him to choose his food even in restaurants. They both claimed that he was unable to choose the type of dishes, pieces and quantities that best suited him. Neither did he ever buy clothes or shoes for himself unless accompanied by her.

On Sundays after Mass she stopped at the best pâtisserie in the area to buy cakes. I have a very painful association with cake buying. In his teens my brother developed worrying symptoms: epileptic fits and loss of power in one leg. Various doctors were consulted. I always accompanied Mamma in these medical errands as she thought that I was better able to deal with professionals. On this particular Sunday morning, I drove her to a private hospital to collect the results of some tests. We were given them by a young doctor who told us that the prognosis was very bad and that she should resign herself to seeing her son become gradually paralyzed. She became distraught, as I had never seen her before. I tried to tell her that the doctor was young and might have made a mistake. Within a quarter of an hour she calmed down and said:

'Let us go and get some good cakes. I do not want anyone to know what we have just learned.'

She was fully composed throughout our lunch and nobody guessed. This was a traumatic period for our family, full of uncertainty and forebodings. Within a year or so, new diagnostic equipment allowed the doctors to find out that Franco had a brain tumour. It was successfully operated on.

Mamma Giulia's cooking: *melanzane alla Calabrese*

This is a summer version of the preserved aubergine dish described above. It is to be eaten cold and within two or three days of preparation. Keep refrigerated.

Slice the *melanzane* in half cross-wise and then in triangular segments. I tend to keep about half the peel in this dish. You will end up with four segments for the top, thinner part and six for the bottom part. Put them in plenty of boiling water (unsalted) and cook for about ten minutes. You should be able to pass the fork through easily but do not let them become too mushy.

Drain them in a colander, preferably one with a flat bottom. The idea from now on is to remove as much as possible of the water absorbed by the aubergines in the boiling process. To achieve this, cover them with a clean cloth. I keep a special one for this operation as it becomes messy and cannot be used for anything else even after washing. Put a weight on top: I use a pan full of water. I usually leave them on my sink to drain overnight. Now, the choice of pan/weight is tricky and relates to the size and shape of the colander. When the pan of water is put on top of the cloth covering the aubergines, it should push them down to squeeze away the liquid. If it is too large it will just sit on the side of the colander, leaving the aubergines full of water. If it is too small some aubergines will move to the sides and will not be squeezed.

I can see you are giving up on this one. Do not; help is at hand, more specifically ... in your hands! Thoroughly wash your hands, take several aubergine pieces between them and squeeze the water out. When most of the water has been drained, by whatever method, place the aubergines on a dish and give them plenty of salt, oil, oregano and garlic. Some chilli will go nicely here. If stored they need turning and mixing occasionally to make sure that the oil does not sit at the bottom but is spread to all the aubergines.

This dish can be used to make appetizers for aperitifs or antipasti. Place a small amount of *melanzane* on a thin slice of baguette, ciabatta or brown bread and serve.

20

Mafia?
Never heard of it

Ha detto cose da far rizzare i capelli: che la mafia esiste,
che e' una potente organizzazione, che controlla tutto ...

He said things to make your hair stand on end: that the mafia exists,
that it is a powerful organization, that it controls everything ...
Leonardo Sciascia

Health was not the only concern for my family in the 1960s. The brothers kept bidding for contracts and gradually won many. Their reputation for competence, delivery times and trustworthiness increased. The news of their success and increased wealth spread to Calabria. Meanwhile in Rome there were often meetings of the brothers behind closed doors. They took place in one of the flats owned by the firm in Piazza Annibaliano and designated as 'the office'. In the other flats, the families' homes, there was a growing sense of unease, with much whispering among worried-looking sisters-in-law.

I do not remember ever hearing the word 'mafia' or even the Calabrian version, *'ndrangheta*, during my childhood years in Delianuova. The historian John Dickie traces the introduction of the name to 1955. My mother occasionally referred to some families as *genti brutti* – the same ugly people to whom her father used to serve drinks in inferior glasses, though careful to avoid being found out. She was usually told by older members of the family not to say things like that. One should just mind one's own business and not show any disrespect to such people.

On occasions someone in the family might say that such and such a person behaved like a *'ndranghitista*. This I always took to be a description of the behaviour of a bully rather than of someone belonging to a special criminal group. In fact, I have the feeling that my impression was correct in the sense that no one would have dared to give accusing labels to people who actually belonged to the local mafia. The word *'ndranghitista* might have been used more as a label of fun than in relation to real mafiosi.

Yet the signs were there all right. They still are. Fear gripped Grandfather Antonino - never the macho type - after a shooting between rival bosses just outside his café in Delianuova. He raised the strength to shut his shop, then took to his bed for a week trembling and lamenting that he was going to die of heart failure. One of my cousins made the most of this adventure. He was passing by and managed to take cover. He later tried to build for himself a heroic reputation, claiming to have single-handedly saved the lives of scores of women and children. But these were not the targets of the shooter, who was settling scores with an old enemy in town.

Another episode I remember very well: commotion and whispering among the adults, lots of people going to and fro in the streets, particularly in the vicinity of a house not far from us and belonging to people we did not seem to be particularly friendly with. A young man of the family had been shot dead in the countryside by his cousin in revenge for the earlier killing of his own father by the young man's father. I was struck by various emotions at this event. Someone had actually killed his own cousin. I kept thinking how terrible it was to kill your own cousin. Worse still was the fact that his own mother had encouraged the killer to take revenge.

Some writers on the mafia, such as John Dickie, have noted the power and influence of strong women on the *'ndrangheta* and other mafia families. Their power is exercised not only via incitement to violent acts but also by having key roles in making strategic decisions or in managing the family and clan finances. Such powerful women was certainly not my experience. All the women I knew were deeply shocked by this event. I was also stunned to see that my sister showed no sign of organizing her usual group for entertainment at the vigil. She understood that this event and the aggrieved and lamenting family were not to be used as opportunities for her amusement.

People seemed to accept that *genti brutti* wage war and often kill each other. But even in my childhood, personal violence was not always confined to the mafia. Violent acts, extortion and intimidation were not discussed in front of us children, but occasionally we might hear of somebody having had their crops or equipment burned. A can of petrol might have appeared overnight in front of your house or shop. There were acts of pure bullying via tacit intimidation. A middle-aged man might approach you and with an avuncular voice advise:

'I heard of some nasty people who are after you and your money. Believe me, I only want to secure the welfare of you and your dear family. We can protect you, your family and your business against these terrible dangers.'

There was no need for violent words or threats. Ordinary people knew that it was dangerous to go against the will of some *genti brutti*.

One particular summer's day I witnessed an incident that left a big impression on me throughout my life. We children were spending the summer in Delianuova and I was just coming back from an errand. I entered Piazza Regina Elena from a side road sloping downhill towards the piazza. This was also the quickest way out from Delianuova to the countryside and the mountains. Suddenly, as though sprung from nowhere, I found near me a young man with a red and sweaty face and bloodshot eyes brandishing a pistol in his hand. Fear gripped me: was he going to shoot me or one of the many people who were strolling unaware in the piazza? There was Nonno Francesco. Would he be shot? The man showed no sign of having noticed me. He frantically looked around and then started running uphill along the side road whence I had just descended.

As I proceeded towards my grandparents' home I could see and feel a rising commotion and agitation in town. I later learned the facts. The young man had just shot dead the *maresciallo dei carabinieri*, the chief of the local *carabinieri*, who was leisurely sipping coffee with friends at an open-air table in a café – not my grandfather Antonino's – along the high street. The young man belonged to a family of mafiosi and some of his brothers had been at large for some time. The story was that the *maresciallo* had made a pact with one of them to let him stay at large in exchange for information. Apparently the *maresciallo* had gone back on his word and this was the day he paid for it.

As a young woman of just over 20 and full of aspirations for a better world, I visited a distant relative during a short holiday period in Delianuova. The family was living in a small house proudly kept immaculate and improved as their circumstances improved. As I entered the house it all looked darker than usual. I looked out of the window and saw ongoing building works to erect an extra floor on the house opposite. It had been a large, dilapidated house kept empty for a long time but had recently been bought by local people. I asked my relative why she and her husband had allowed their own house to be spoiled by the construction of an extra storey.

'Well, what could we do? They just went ahead and built.'

'You should complain to the council. If you want I will draft a letter for you.'

She immediately got up and shut the window:

'Shh, shh, keep your voice down. Do not go around saying silly things. With such people it is better to say nothing. Your fancy ideas cannot be applied in Calabria. Anyway, don't worry, it's not so bad. They have not taken a piece of my house, just some light.'

Is it all in the past? Far from it. A family friend who with his family had left Delianuova long ago recently put the paternal house up for sale. There were three reasonable offers. Then a local boss spread the rumour that he was interested in buying it. All three offers were withdrawn. He then made a ridiculously low offer and got it.

Delianuova was a relatively minor outpost of the *'ndrangheta*. The really big shots were somewhere else. As a child I had heard that all the big 'ugly men' would meet towards the end of August in

16. Edward Lear's drawing of Santa Maria di Polsi in 1847

the mountains, at the festival of the Madonna della Montagna. The Madonna di Polsi had long been a place of religious pilgrimage. John Dickie dates to 1894 the earliest record of meetings of mafia bosses in this remote village up on the Aspromonte massif. Polsi and its Madonna had captured the imagination of Edward Lear some 47 years earlier. This remote monastery, now associated with one of the most intractable social problems of Calabria, was considered by Lear as the most remarkable site he had ever seen. He produced one of his best drawings on the Aspromonte.

Traditionally the Polsi meetings became the occasion for the settling of mafia business and scores. Almost every year somebody was shot dead. A female relative of my mother's commented:

'Once again they have killed somebody. It happens every year. Maybe the Madonna wants these sacrifices. After all it is not such a bad thing if they shoot each other.'

But settling of scores is not the main reason for these annual meetings of the top *'ndrangheta* bosses. This is when major decisions are collectively taken and promotions dished out, according to Dickie. The organization has a hierarchical structure, with trusted men making their way up from Santa to Vangelo to Madre Santissima (Most Holy Mother). These titles are a reflection of the strong links between mafia people and religion. Traditional mafiosi wanted to be – and be seen as – devout and operating within the folds of the Catholic Church. This partly accounts for a strange, long-established practice.

Most Italian villages celebrate their patron saint or madonna with a procession, as described in Chapter 9. In many villages of Calabria, Campania and Sicily the statue is taken on a small detour to the houses of well-known and powerful mafia bosses. The bearers cause the statue to pause or even make a small bow in front of the house. From his balcony, the boss, surrounded by his family and friends, bows to the madonna. Some local priests and bishops have occasionally connived in this. Most have done so out of fear. This bizarre practice might be seen as humorous were it not for the fact that it is quite sinister. Why is the saint or madonna made to pay homage to the boss? Does the boss ask that the statue be brought to him and his family so that they can pay – and be seen to pay – homage to Catholicism? Either way there is a show of power. The madonna statue is made to go the bosses' way in defiance of the power of the Church and state. The direct representatives of these two institutions, the priests and the *carabinieri*, are always in the first line of the procession. Recently some *carabinieri* abandoned the procession at the detour point in protest at what they were forced to witness. The defiance to the established power takes place in front of the whole village. Who among the villagers dares defy such an in-your-face show of power?

The pope can and Pope Francis has recently done it. He has made clear in various speeches that Catholicism and the mafia are incompatible. All people involved in mafia activities have been excommunicated en masse. Following his pronouncements, in 2015 several bishops have forbidden the procession in villages known to have followed this practice in the past. The prohibitions have not gone down well with the local shopkeepers, who see the enthusiasm for the festivities as well as their sales declining. A suggestion has been made that the names of young people allowed to carry the statue be chosen at random or that well-known mafiosi youth be excluded as bearers.

It is an unfortunate misconception that the mafia thrives partly due to so-called *omertà*, the alleged connivance of the local population – a misconception fuelled partly by politicians who do not want to stare the facts in the face and take action. It is true that on the whole the local population does not report abuse to themselves or to others; neither do they come forward as witnesses when called upon. But then they know that, given the mafia links to sections of the police and politicians, their complaints and evidence are likely to be reported back to the mafia bosses. The outcome would be great danger and suffering for themselves and their families while the mafia would be hardly affected. It is not collusion that keeps the majority of the population from speaking. It is fear. The mafia problem in southern Italy is largely a problem of the political class, the state institutions and their power in postwar Italy.

PART III
DELIANUOVA. HAVE I EVER LEFT IT?

21

International affairs

There was plenty to see; nearly all the life of Cambridge
flowed backwards and forwards over our bridge ...
Gwen Raverat

The omens were good. I met Donald in Cambridge on St Valentine's Day in 1970. Things progressed quite fast on the emotional level, though not much research into the philosophy of science or economics was done for the rest of the year. We soon decided he should come to Italy and meet the family – a scary experience for someone who has a total of four first cousins rarely met. We spent a couple of weeks with my sister, her husband and little Francesca in Moena in the Dolomites before heading for Rome.

After parking the car, we made our way to the Ietto flats. Before we arrived we met Papà. He hardly said a word and proceeded to walk towards home ahead of us. This was quite out of character. In a worried state, I asked Mamma whether this was a sign that he had taken against Donald.

'Nonsense. He has just had a tooth out and is afraid of cutting a poor show in front of your friend.'

Within an hour or so of our arrival the doorbell started ringing. Aunts and cousins came cautiously. They apparently needed to borrow an onion or some garlic or a bunch of parsley or a torch. A look at the young Englishman, some remarks about how amazing it was that he understood Italian and off they went with an onion or garlic or some parsley.

Back in Cambridge we decided to get married. Donald, on a further charm offensive, drafted a letter to my parents and asked me to correct his Italian. I left some mistakes in to make it look more authentic. They were delighted. When I went back for Christmas we discussed the ceremony and celebrations. My wish for a civil wedding did not create a stir or murmur from my immediate family. They said that as the husband-to-be was a foreigner and had different beliefs, we should respect them. I suspect that they may also have felt that, as educated people, we knew better. In any case the Campidoglio seemed an impressive enough location for a wedding.

The old heart problem was never far away from my mind and before Christmas I consulted a cardiologist at Hammersmith Hospital in London. He suggested a diagnostic catheterization. We fixed it for the next January, before the wedding which was scheduled for February. It emerged that my heart had a congenital stenosis. It was remarkable that I had not shown serious heart problems given the size of the restriction. I was told to expect problems in the years to come unless the restriction was removed surgically. Donald and I decided to think about it and to get in touch with the consultant after the wedding.

The catheterization was not without its problems. A small clot developed in the upper leg where the catheter was inserted. My brother came to see me through it and to help me back to Rome. The recovery took much longer than anticipated and the wedding had to be postponed. Hundreds of notes had to be sent out announcing the cancellation and re-scheduling due to ill health. In Italy weddings are announced to a very large constituency, only some of which are invited with a special card placed inside the main 'participation' card. Shortly after the cancellation notes were sent out, telephone calls and visits started coming in. The mother of one of my aunts came to seek assurance about my health and the wedding. She was puzzled about the venue of the wedding.

'I never heard of such weddings before. They are not real weddings, are they? But, on the other hand, you are over 30 and it is better to get this type of wedding than none at all.'

Unknown to me rumours spread from Rome to Calabria and back.

'Poor girl! She trusted a foreigner and he jilted her. Never mind, she has her job and interest in her studies. Marriage was not really for someone like her, was it?'

We proved them wrong. The wedding took place on 4 April.

The heart operation was fixed for May 1972, some 13 months after the wedding. Mamma arrived a few days before the event. More than once I discovered her crying and had to console her and reassure her that all would be well. While I was in hospital my brother and father arrived. Angela, pregnant with Giulia, remained behind. Donald coped with the three of them and the inevitable cultural differences. Mamma took over the kitchen and the running of the small, furnished flat we were renting in Ealing, West London.

Immediately after the operation only my husband was allowed to enter the recovery room to see me. Whoever wrote the hospital rules did not reckon with my mother's determination. She demanded to be allowed to see her daughter with her own eyes. In she went. Out she came totally distraught.

Things did not go well. The restriction was even bigger than anticipated and the lungs were flooded. I remained suspended between life and death for almost a week. Two reminiscences emerged later from that semi-lost period. Both were regressions to my childhood. One day when Donald was visiting I looked pleased and sported a childish smile. I told him of some lovely custard I had been offered. The other one was linguistic. The doctors and nurses, naturally, talked to me in English. The effort to understand what they were saying remained with me for a long time. I felt that I had to make some kind of translation first into Italian and then into Calabrese before comprehending what was being said to me. The Calabrese dialect came back to my mind with more ease and a stronger feeling of reassurance than Italian or English.

Back in the ward I received daily visits from Donald and Mamma. The two of them got on well. She taught Donald how to cook Italian dishes so that he could look after her daughter when she came home. Mamma left London after four weeks and came back when I was finally ready to go home. Meanwhile doctors and nurses took excellent care of me for a total of seven weeks in

Hammersmith Hospital followed by two weeks in a countryside convalescent home.

On her return after my discharge Mamma arrived loaded with food, some already cooked and some not. She brought her own supply of garlic and parsley. By the time she was back she was already familiar with the local shops near Gunnersbury Park. The green-grocer reviewed his policy on the touching of wares by customers when faced with this demanding but discerning foreigner. They communicated with gestures just as the butcher and baker did. Language barriers were no obstacle to her bringing back to our Ealing home the best available provisions and making friends with the shopkeepers.

To ensure full recovery, I postponed by a year the start of the academic job I had been offered before the operation. The full emotional recovery – the end of the 'heart problem' – came with the birth of Mark in 1975, three years after the operation. At that point Mamma switched to worrying about her grandson and about my own life and future. She would often ring up to enquire about us and to urge me to go back to work because:

' ... in the years to come you will not be happy unless you use your education. Working only at home is what any uneducated woman like me can do. You must do more.'

Mamma Giulia's cooking: mixed vegetables for a summer evening

Peperonata: the real thing, my mother's way

You need one or two aubergines, three or four peppers, possibly of different colours, a couple of courgettes, seeded, peeled and chopped-up tomatoes, and an onion cut into segments. Mamma always used fresh San Marzano tomatoes. In London, I use the tinned variety.

Cut the aubergines into small chunks, approximately 2½cm cubed, leaving the peel on all of them. Remove stalks and seeds from the peppers and cut them into pieces of about 2½cm square.

Cut the courgettes into similar-sized chunks.

Fry the vegetables in separate oil, either in different pans or sequentially in the same pan after removing the oil and wiping the pan clean. In a separate large frying pan – or the same one wiped of previous oil and frying debris – put a very small amount of oil and lightly fry the onion. Add chopped tomatoes and let them cook for a few minutes. Add your aubergines, peppers and courgettes. Mix all the vegetables together and cook for two to three minutes. For a more filling dish you can add potatoes cut in oblong slices, fried separately and then added to the other vegetables with the onions and tomatoes.

Second best: *peperonata with fewer calories and less labour*

I have developed an easier version of *peperonata*: easier on your time and effort and on calories. Prepare the aubergines, peppers and courgettes as above. I also add potatoes cut to about 3cm cubed. Put everything into a baking tray and add onions (at least two cut in largish segments) and a lot of chopped tomatoes. Sprinkle with salt, add a good amount of oil and stir. Bake at 220 degrees for about an hour, stirring occasionally. It is easy to prepare, makes a good show for a party and tastes very good, though not as good as my mother's version.

Verdure arrosto in bianco

A different version of the *peperonata* above can be achieved by preparing the vegetables to be baked without the addition of tomatoes. They need a little extra oil. The finished product is very tasty. They can be stored in the fridge for longer than the tomato variety.

22

Tragedy in the family

Say good-bye to your father. You won't see him again, dear.
He died too young, before his time ...
Maxim Gorky

The heart operation was not the only distress my parents endured in the months and years after the joy of my wedding. It was a sunny May morning less than two months after our nuptials. Cambridge was at its best. We were still living in a rented room in a lovely house in Barton Road. Donald was working out his fellowship at King's and waiting to move to his new job at Chelsea College, London, in the autumn. The phone rang and the landlady's maid came in to tell me that it was someone speaking a foreign language. It might be for me. It was. From Rome. Zio Mimmo had been shot during a kidnapping attempt in Calabria. He was being transferred by plane to a Rome hospital. He died within a month, leaving three children and a pregnant widow.

It came as a shock and yet not entirely as a surprise. Within the family, mafia issues were never discussed in front of women, no matter whether they were educated or not. I never heard them discussed even when I became a young and not-so-young woman. Yet I knew that the Ietto brothers moved to Rome with their families driven by pull-and-push forces: the pull of larger contracts in the capital and the push of an ever more exacting mafia. More recently, through hushed voices, I understood that something very worrying had happened on the Calabrian road from Reggio to Delianuova. The youngest of my uncles was returning home one evening when a couple of *carabinieri* armed with rifles stopped him. They asked him to get out of the car and follow them for routine checks. His immediate reaction was:

'You are not *carabinieri*' and he sped away.

His intuition was based on the accent of the so-called *carabinieri*. They were speaking with a very unlikely Calabrian accent. Usually *carabinieri* are posted far away from their own regions to avoid connivance and corruption.

By the time I got married in 1971, all the families had moved and one uncle, Mimmo, was going back and forth trying to wind up the last pieces of business in Calabria. Unfortunately he left it too late. One evening when driving home from Reggio along the mountain road he was stopped by armed men who attempted to kidnap him. He was not one for submitting easily and was shot in the spine. He was the one who had shown a keen interest in my supply teacher and the one who had often told me how much he missed the lack of opportunities to study. He used to take advantage of any reading material that came his way and was also very fond of opera.

My father took the whole episode very badly. He used to talk about it incessantly and never let a week pass without going to the cemetery to lay flowers on his brother's tomb. He died four years later of a brain haemorrhage at the age of 63. I am sure that the grief and anger at the violent death of his brother was a strong contributory factor in his own early death.

A few weeks after his funeral two of the brothers were visiting the cemetery. They stopped for flowers from a stall just outside the gates. The florist asked:

'There is a man who used to come every Sunday morning to visit the tomb of his brother who had been killed. I have not seen him for a while. I think he is your brother. Anything wrong?'

On learning of his death, she told them how sad she felt. He always had a few words with her while buying flowers. She gave them a bunch to be put on his grave from her.

'Up and down Italy, around 650 citizens were kidnapped by crimi-
nals in the 1970s and 1980s,' writes John Dickie. Most of these
crimes were perpetrated by mafia groups. The *'ndrangheta* played a
big part in them. Their control of the Aspromonte mountains gave
them excellent hiding places for both their victims and themselves.
Most kidnapping was done locally, though a few victims were taken
in other parts of Italy. These were the ones that usually made the
headlines. Zio Mimmo's was an exceptional case. He made it into
the national media because of the violence involved and his death.
The biggest media case, however, was that of Paul Getty's grandson. One of his ears was cut off and sent to the family as proof of
his detention.

Kidnapping became big mafia business in the 1970s and early
1980s. It was a departure from their activities during the previous two decades. These were largely based on extracting money
from local small businesses which were growing fast as part of the
general economic development of Italy. It was also facilitated by
inefficient and occasionally conniving state institutions.

The centre and north of Italy were growing much faster than
the south. The opportunities of exploitation by the mafia were
enormous. But it could not easily be done via extortion – the fear
factor was not as deep-rooted as in the south. Kidnapping became
the answer. When, eventually, a law was passed by the Italian parlia-
ment for the freezing of assets of the family of kidnapped victims,
the game was up. The mafia had to change strategy. They went
into drugs. This caused their activities to spread much wider and,
indeed, globally. But mafia families tend to be still very localized
within the three traditional regions of operation. One beneficial
effect of this is that the drugs trade has been less pronounced in
these regions and elsewhere in Italy. So is petty crime. The bosses
seem to be more efficient at keeping their regions, peoples and
visiting tourists safe than the regular Italian police.

Papà used to rant against democracy, the Christian Democrats and
the communists.

'Mussolini was wrong to wage all those wars and ally himself
with Hitler. But remember, Grazia, there was no mafia when he

was in power. He got rid of them all.'

'Oh! The scoundrel. He even took our gold wedding rings to pay for his war! We had to buy new ones after the war,' was Mamma's comment.

As I argued with him on the advantages of democracy he would tell me that most of the people up there were sheltering, aiding – and being aided by – the mafia in the south. Six months after the death of his brother he sent a long telegram to several high-level politicians warning them of links between the mafia and politics and inviting them to clean things up. He received no answer but he was pleased to have let off steam and to have expressed his disgust. We only learned about these telegrams after he sent them and I read a draft copy after he died. Amidst some grammatical mistakes, the emotional outpouring comes out in every line and still makes painful reading.

Years later he and his brother Gianni were proposed for a special commendation for services to the economy. His brother was awarded a title without any problems. For him, however, there was much dilly-dallying. Eventually he was told, confidentially, that there was something against him in the police archives. He was led to believe that those telegrams were indeed the problem. Eventually Papà received official recognition. He never boasted about it and rarely mentioned it.

The Calabrian mafia dates back to after the unification of Italy in 1861. Some claim that it was a way of introducing order into the chaos left by the state, which was seen as too remote and uninterested in the destiny of the Calabrian people. Placanica notes how, in the following decades, the Calabrian provinces with the highest numbers of brigands were also the ones with the highest numbers of migrants.

Mussolini did, indeed, give a big knock to the mafia. It began to thrive again through the running of the black market during the war. After the war it was on the back of politics. The years immediately after World War II saw the destiny of Italy suspended between moves towards communism or liberal democracy. The Christian Democrats, with the support of the American government, wanted to make sure that Italy moved in the second direction. In southern Italy the mafia was enlisted to help shift the balance of political power. It did. At a cost. It started a sinister collaboration between political power and the mafia that continues to this day, with a few glimmers of hope on the horizon.

Following Zio Mimmo's death the Ietto brothers and their families go to Delianuova only for weddings and funerals.

23

Going back

The familiar land beckons me ...
as I hear the song of the Calabrian peasant,
and see the colours on mountain and on sea.
George Gissing

I did go back in 1993. For many years I had been longing to return and show Donald and Mark the small town I came from. They wanted to see the site of the many stories they had heard from me.

At Reggio airport we were met by Zio Micu Scutellà and his son Renato, a high-school teacher. Via Marina, the traditional town jewel, was our first sight. It was as stunning as ever. The unregulated building developments that had defaced much of Reggio had been less brutal on this town landmark. Several attractive art nouveau houses still grace it. So do palm trees. Not much is left of what had been built before the 1908 earthquake. Norman Douglas, who visited the area shortly after the quake, gave a moving account of the destruction he saw. His feelings for a region and a people he loved come alive in what is one of the best chapters in his book. The 'Macello', the town slaughterhouse that so astonished Gissing, was also destroyed. In Gissing's own words:

> I found myself approaching what looked like a handsome public edifice, a museum or gallery of art. It was a long building, graced with a portico, and coloured effectively in dull red; all about it stood lemon trees, and behind, overtopping the roof, several fine palms.

Often enough in its long history Reggio has paid a high price for its strategic and geographical position. Incursions from both the Tyrrhenian and the Ionian seas were always a problem in earlier centuries and earthquakes have shaken its foundations on many – too many – occasions. Yet its position remains as magnificent as ever. An amphitheatre rising steeply over the Aspromonte hills, it affords wonderful views over the Straits of Messina and, on your left, Etna itself. Its sight more than compensates for the high winds hitting the town from many directions and for the black dust that occasionally covers your furniture, floors and balconies. You can make the best of it by gathering the black intruder and pouring it over your basil, parsley and lemon plants.

Renato drove on. My negative view of the topiaries in Via Garibaldi had not changed from my first visit at the age of eight. Time to go to the museum. Zio Micu kept the most recent town jewel last. With great pride he took us to see I Bronzi di Riace. He was not the only member of the extended family to show interest and pride in these two sculptures. In June 1982 Mamma rang me up in London:

'Grazia, they are fantastic. I have never seen anything so beautiful.'

'What, Mamma, what are you talking about?'

'Oh! I Bronzi di Riace. They are in Rome on their way to Reggio. They were in Florence for restoration. I have seen them. I had to queue, but it was well worth it. They are big. They seem real. So impressive. You must go and see them.'

She was right. They are impressive. Two perfect, naked warriors, proud and with faces graced by curly hair and beards. In August 1972 a Roman chemist on holiday was scuba diving near Riace in the Ionian Sea when he saw what looked like an arm sticking out from the sea floor. The two statues were later recovered. We were luckier than Lee Langley. 'For half a lifetime I've wanted to see the Riace bronzes,' writes the novelist. She could only see them while in restoration, sealed off by a glass wall, 'supine, cradled in protective wooden crossbeams, not resplendent, but fallen warriors, touching in their vulnerability'.

This chance discovery gave the world of classical scholars a

17. I Bronzi di Riace

great new interest to focus on. The warriors have been dated back
to some two and half millennia ago. They are definitely Greek in
conception, beauty and artistry. But being Greek does not mean
they were actually conceived and made in what we now know as
Greece. They may have been made in what is now Calabria. The
area where they were found, near Locri, so dear to George Gissing,
was part of Greece. So was the hamlet where I was born. Paracorio – a derivative Greek name meaning 'the small town over the
mountain' – was established by people from the Greek town of
Delia near the current Bova.

   As we were about to leave the museum, Zio Micu rushed back
and returned shortly with small copies of the two statues for us
to take back to London. They now stand on a shelf in my study
– a reminder of this kind and generous uncle. A sumptuous
lunch awaited us at their home. In the afternoon we set off for
Delianuova. The roads were better this time and I did not suffer
car sickness. What I saw along the Costa Viola, the Purple Coast,

was more stunning than I remembered. After years of familiarity with the English countryside, the sight of houses huddled together or perched up on improbable slopes and rocky terrain struck me as it had never done before.

Past Scilla and Bagnara we headed inland towards the hills. Large expanses of olive groves awaited us: their size and magnificence was just what I remembered. Zio Micu and Renato took us on a little detour to drink at a mountain spring, water so good, fresh and tasty that:

'Grazia, it might almost resuscitate the dead.'

Our reception at Delianuova was no less warm and generous. The meals were excellent. Talking to Zio Rocco and Zia Angelina, now aged, was a treat. Their kindness towards their nephews and nieces that I remembered so well was now extended to my son. We were offered delicious cakes and delicacies. I longed, as I had done for decades, to taste Zio Rocco's crusty edges of *Pan di Spagna* mixed with leftover custard. I was offered the best. I felt too embarrassed to ask for what I really wanted. Zio Rocco, now into his 80s, showed us his new wonder machine: an electric oven introduced by his son Nino. He was, at first, very suspicious of such advanced technology and kept talking with nostalgia of the wonderful open-fire oven built for him by his childhood friends, my father and his brother Gianni when they were all young. It had worked efficiently for decades. Why change to unknown methods? When he saw the results of the new oven, however, he became reconciled to it but he insisted that he should be the one to press the 'On' button and start the baking process.

The gratification of my taste buds had to wait until my next visit in 2009 when I became bolder with Zio Rocco's grandson, also called Rocco. He is now in charge of the business. He is as keen as his grandfather to improve himself and the business and keep its high reputation. He is the first Calabrese whose work and business has been recognized by the prestigious Accademia Maestri Pasticceri Italiani. Rocco offered us the best cakes and pastries for our breakfast. I asked for the outside, overcooked bits of the *Pan di Spagna*. He obliged and I had the most wonderful experience. Vivid memories of childhood Sunday lunches engulfed me.

18. Zii Rocco and Angelina in their pastry workshop.
Visited by Grazia, Donald and Mark in 1993

Mamma Giulia's cooking: *melanzane* forever

The basis for several dishes: melanzane fritte o grigliate

Cut the *melanzane* lengthwise in slices about ⅓cm thick. No peeling is necessary except for the two outside slices. From these, remove all peel except for the contour. Fry the slices in about 1cm of oil, turning them once. When taking them out of the pan place them on fat-absorbing paper.

Alternatively you can grill them at about 200 degrees for five to six minutes on each side. You can brush a little oil on them but it is not necessary. The frying process gives you more tender and tasty dishes. However, the grilling process absorbs less fat. The grilled aubergines can be dressed with garlic, oregano and oil and served on their own. They are good served together with other grilled vegetables – *grigliata mista* – such as courgettes or radicchio. Grilled aubergines can also be used as the basis for other dishes such as the following.

Melanzane con il pomodoro

In a frying pan put some chopped-up fresh ripe tomatoes, or tinned if the fresh ones are not available. No added oil is necessary. Let them cook for a few minutes. Meanwhile shred the aubergine slices into small pieces. Add them to the tomatoes and let them cook together for four or five minutes. Add basil and a small amount of salt. You can use grilled aubergines instead with the addition of some oil if the grilled *melanzane* have not been pre-oiled. On a summer day I often serve this dish as an accompaniment to a simple meat or fish dish. It can be served as a vegetable or as an excellent condiment for pasta. In the latter case, the shredded *melanzane* can be added directly to the tomato sauce. On a gorgeous summer day of 2007 this was one of the most appreciated vegetables I prepared for four Japanese friends, philosophers of science from Kyoto University visiting Donald.

Parmigiana di melanzane

The Greek version of this dish is known as *moussaka*. You can start with either fried or grilled *melanzane* slices. The fried *melanzane* give a better result, though the number of calories will be higher. You also need a simple tomato sauce, as described in Chapter 5. Use an oven dish and lay a first layer of cooked *melanzane* slices; then put in a layer of chopped mozzarella cheese followed by a layer of tomato sauce. Choose mozzarella which is not watery but hard. You can substitute mild cheddar for mozzarella. The top layer should be aubergines and tomato sauce. If the aubergines are grilled you may need a little oil at the bottom of the dish and you could put a little oil in each layer, though it is not absolutely necessary because there will be some oil in the tomato sauce. On the very top you can put a little grated parmesan cheese. Bake in a hot oven for half an hour.

A richer version of this can be achieved by using Napoletana tomato sauce which contains minced meat. An even richer one can be made by putting layers of chopped-up hard-boiled eggs on top of the mozzarella cheese. In my view the best one is the simplest and least rich one.

These dishes can also be made with *zucchine* sliced in long thin strips.

Melanzane al funghetto

Cut the *melanzane* lengthwise in half and then each half in two or three sections lengthwise. Then slice each section in small cubes of about 2cm. Each section will have peel on it. Fry in about 1cm of hot oil. It takes a few minutes. When they start colouring they are ready to go on the fat-absorbing paper. Dress with garlic, oregano and parsley and serve as a vegetable. You can also add them to tomato sauce and use this as a condiment for pasta.

A slightly different version of this dish, less rich in calories, is obtained by frying the aubergine cubes for only a couple of minutes in very little oil, just enough to grease your pan. Stir often. In a separate pan, lightly fry some chopped onions and add chopped tomatoes and then the aubergine cubes. Let them cook together for some 10-15 minutes. You can use this dish as vegetables or as a condiment for pasta or rice.

24

You can't cook decent meals without olive oil

... la cucina mi pareva allora rischiarata da una luce angelica ...
i miei sogni ... mi condussero quasi sempre a spaziare nelle cucine.

... the kitchen seemed to be lit up with an angelic glow ...
my dreams almost always take place in kitchens.
Ippolito Nievo

The meals we were offered during our visit to Delianuova, though more sumptuous, were not very different from the ones Mamma cooked for us in Rome. She added some Roman touches to her Calabrian cooking. My move to London gave my parents their only direct contact with international and exotic cuisine. Cultural misunderstandings started to pile up.

A few weeks before the wedding I mentioned that Ross, Donald's mother, had started making a large wedding cake. It was to be eaten at the post-wedding party that she and her husband Fyfe were organizing in Cambridge for our British friends. Mamma was horrified:

'A cake two months ahead?' Oh! It will poison everybody. I must tell all my family not to touch it.'

On the day they all enjoyed it and she was amazed at the different customs. Indeed she later became very complimentary about Ross's excellent culinary abilities.

'She cooks the meat and vegetables differently from us. But it all comes out very tasty.'

Mamma took enthusiastically to English Cox's apples.

'You know, Grazia, it is curious but the apples taste much better here than in Rome.'

When in later years I would ask what she would like me to bring her from London, the answer was almost always:

'Oh! Bring me some of those little sourish apples. They are so tasty!'

I took a few in February 2003 when I went to Rome alarmed at the deterioration in her health. She never improved enough to eat even one. They were left in a basket in the kitchen terrace among the items Angela and I cleared out after her death.

Ross and her family were very well disposed towards their Italian daughter-in-law. For years they had had holidays in Venice and had read widely about Italian art and history. They also enjoyed Italian food and Ross tried her hand at it. One day she made lasagne for the family lunch. She started reminiscing about a particular visit to Italy. On the train taking them back to Britain she got into conversation with a pleasant Italian woman. The latter tried to explain, in Italian, how to make the egg pasta for lasagne. Out of the blue she mentioned putting the pasta on the bed. At this point in the conversation Ross thought that she must have misunderstood. How could a bed have anything to do with cooking?

'Grazia, all these years I have been wondering what the lady meant when she mentioned bed or a word similar to it. Is there a similar word used in cooking?'

'Oh no! The word she used was bed. Your Italian was and is fine. The bed is relevant in the pasta-making process.'

Italian women usually make egg pasta on special days when they have a large party of family and friends. Several large layers of egg pasta have to be prepared and each one must be laid to rest and dry while the next one is being spread with the rolling pin. Now, if you are an Italian housewife, you are working your pasta with the rolling pin on the kitchen table and you have already set the main table for dinner, so the only remaining large, flat surface is your bed. You lay a large clean cloth on it and put your pasta layers on the bed as you make them. This is what Zia Velia used to do in Delianuova and later in Rome or at Tor San Lorenzo.

One gorgeous summer Mamma was visiting us in our first owned flat, on an estate in Ealing. Dandelions were growing on the communal lawn all around our ground-floor flat. She saw them and went out with a kitchen knife and a bag and started collecting them. Donald asked me what she was doing. On hearing of her intention to cook the dandelions he became very alarmed at the possibility that they might be poisonous. I tried to dissuade her but she took no notice. She reminded me how she used to gather them in the Delianuova countryside during the war to provide food for her family. She cooked them as she used to do in Calabria: a thick soup of dandelions, potatoes and courgettes, as described in Chapter 19. They made a delicious meal which she and I ate under Donald's worried look. He was amused to see a recent article by James Wong in the *Observer Magazine* hailing the virtues of a newly discovered vegetable: dandelions. They have been known and eaten for a long time in France, Italy, China and India. At last they are being introduced into Britain.

Dandelions can also be served as a vegetable. Boil them with the addition of salt. They take some 20 minutes. Drain most of the water from them. You can squeeze them between your hands when they cool down. In a frying pan with a generous amount of olive oil, cook some chopped garlic and add the dandelions. Turn and mix a couple of times. The addition of some chilli goes well with this dish.

The most important ingredient for the dandelion dishes and for all Calabrian ones is good olive oil. From her very first visit to London Mamma realized that olive oil was in short supply there. It worried her. In Delianuova olive oil played a key role in cooking but also served as a status symbol. One sign of your position in the community was whether you had to buy your oil by the litre or whether you had enough land to produce oil for your family or for sale or whether you had enough cash to buy the annual supply needed by your family all in one go. Neither of the two sides of my family was ever a landowner. However, with the first financial successes of his sons, my grandfather bought a smallish holding, enough to provide oil for his increasing extended family. It was enough for all the Ietto households for many years.

When we were next in Rome, as a married couple, one morning she came back from her shopping expedition bearing a ten-litre plastic container and proceeded to clean it thoroughly.

'Mamma, what is this container for?'

'It is for you. To take oil to London. You can't cook decent meals without good olive oil.'

We bought a special travel bag and took Calabrian oil as part of the hand luggage. We stopped this practice when the container developed a leak. Moreover, as years went by, the family supply of Calabrian oil ran out. The tenant farmer declared that the trees had become barren and the plot almost worthless. He bought it.

Olive oil was not the only food we took to London. When the time approached for our departure from Rome Mamma would telephone Domenico, her trusted butcher, and give her instructions:

'Domenico, I need a couple of kilos of your very good sausages. I specially entrust this commission to you, Domenico. I want the very best sausages. They are for Grazia and her English husband to take to London. You know, they do not have such good ones there.'

During the BSE crisis in Britain, when there was fear that it might be spreading to the rest of Europe, I urged her to be more selective on the type of meat she bought. She reminded me that,

'I only buy it from Domenico and he would never give me infected meat!'

So she carried on with her usual meat supply including *ossi buco* and other bone steaks. When, after the death of my father, she moved away from the area, she would still go once a week to buy her meat at Domenico's and then visit her trusted hairdresser. When she could no longer travel, Franco was given the task of collecting the meat she had ordered by phone. He took it to her during his usual visits on Saturday afternoons.

While on a recent visit to Rome I visited Domenico, the old family butcher, and bought meat from him. Though aged and with poor eyesight he is still keen on his job and still carves meat with the loving hand of an artist. He and his wife were delighted to see me and to reminisce about Mamma:

'Oh, there are no more customers like her! She knew about meat and she wanted the best. She always asked about our daughters and how they were doing. We miss her.'

Once, when visiting us in London, Mamma noticed that frozen food was much more common there than in Rome. She did not trust it:

'It is not natural for food to be reduced to such a stony state.'

Similarly she distrusted out-of-season vegetables. When I tried to explain that the vegetables and fruit come to London from the southern hemisphere, she replied:

'But it is not natural for aubergines and peppers to travel that distance. They cannot be really good.'

In those years when I went back and forth between London and Rome with my new family there was a great deal of cooking activity, but there was no question of anybody else doing it: Mamma did not wish it and none of us dared to compare ourselves with her. Angela and I hardly ever cooked in our parental home as long as she was alive. Yet we learned partly from watching her and partly from knowing what good food should taste like. Both Angela and I developed an interest in cooking after Mamma's death.

She could never give us precise details on any of her recipes, but I gradually developed ways of extracting information.

'Mamma how long would you cook the chicken for?'

'Well, I'm not sure; you know, just leave it on the hob/oven till it is ready.'

'What, Mamma, two hours?'

'Two hours? What are you saying? No, no, you will dry it out. Not two hours!'

'Twenty minutes then?'

'Oh no, it would not be enough. A little longer.'

'Half an hour?'

'Yes, more or less. But it all depends how tough the chicken is and how big the pieces. You really have to keep an eye on your cooking to see when it is ready.'

It is not that she did not want to tell us. She really was not into precision. Because she spent the whole morning in the kitchen she was always checking on her food. She did not have a kitchen clock and did not see the need for one. In later years she tried harder to explain the details of her cooking to my son. She was amazed at his interest and skills in cooking. She had to be more precise than with her daughters. As a boy, details of cooking procedures did not come naturally to him.

Alas! Food and cooking became the biggest problem for her and her children in old age. The isolation brought on by deafness further contributed to her fixation on what she was best at: caring for her family and cooking. However, she never got used to the idea of cooking for one person only. As a series of small strokes made her increasingly forgetful, she would go out over and over again to buy food of which there was already plenty in the fridge. She cooked large amounts and urged children, grandchildren and their partners to collect meals from her. Sometimes she gave delicious dishes to shop assistants who had been particularly nice to her, to friendly church-goers, to workmen who might come to make repairs in her flat, to her doctor. Whenever Donald, Mark and I visited, she was delighted and felt in charge of her cooking again. Unfortunately, after the first day or two the excess of food which we felt obliged to eat became too much.

In her last two years she was looked after by a Polish lady to whom she became attached. At first she was reluctant to have anyone in her home but she soon took the line that the Polish carer was a poor woman away from her home and Mamma felt that she had to look after her by cooking delicious meals.

Unfortunately she also started eating too much. She had never been fat. A little on the plump side perhaps, but not fat. In her old age she put on a considerable amount of weight and this undermined her health. Years earlier she had prepared the clothes she wanted to be dressed in when she died. She laid out high-quality underwear, stockings and slip to be used on her dead body. As regards the exterior she thought that any of her many suits could be used. She showed me these items and instructed me many years before the event. But by the time she needed them they had become too small for her.

Our last visits were sad. She was overweight and unable to stop food shopping, cooking and eating. I could also see that this was all becoming too much for her. I realized that her end was not far away when, on my very last visit before her final illness, I saw that she had delegated the cooking to Dora, her Polish carer.

Mamma Giulia's cooking: delicacies for aperitifs or as antipasto

In our more affluent period Mamma prepared the following as aperitif nibbles – i.e. to eat with a little wine before a meal. We never had proper aperitifs. These canapés are also delicious as side vegetables. They are at their best still hot and crispy. Other good canapés for aperitifs are: *carciofi fritti dorati* (Chapter 16), aubergines or meat and aubergine fritters (Chapter 10), and *melanzane alla Calabrese* served on small slices of bread (Chapter 19).

Frittelle di cavolfiore

Boil cauliflower florets till fully cooked. Drain them and cut into small pieces or mash lightly with a fork. Separately prepare a batter in the normal way with an egg, flour and milk. Put the cauliflower into the batter and stir. Sprinkle with salt. Take spoonfuls of this mixture and fry in hot oil some 2cm deep; turn once. Remove when they turn golden in colour. Place on fat-absorbing paper. They tend to come out as irregular oval shapes of about 3x4cm.

Fiori di zucchine

The flowers from courgettes have a pleasing appearance with their lily shape and yellow/orange colour touched by streaks of white and green. More importantly they make very tasty dishes. They were among my mother's favourites. You can buy them in Italy but unfortunately I have never seen them on sale in Britain. I often wonder what happens to the courgette flowers. I hope they are not discarded. Here are some dishes in case you are able to get them.

Frittelle di fiori di zucchine

There is no need to pre-cook the flowers, just remove the stamens and the spiky green sepals. Cut them in small pieces and follow the procedure as for *frittelle di cavolfiore*. Dip them into a batter and mix. Fry them and place on the usual kitchen paper to absorb the excess fat.

Fiori di zucchine con mozzarella e acciughe

Remove the stamens and green sepals but leave the flower whole. Put inside each a small amount of mozzarella cheese and a little bit of anchovy fillet. Dip in a light batter – not too thick – and fry. Place on fat-absorbent paper.

Bruschetta

This is an antipasto now available in many restaurants in Italy and beyond. Cut fresh tomatoes into small pieces. I like to use ripe, succulent tomatoes. I peel, seed and cut them. Leave for half an hour to allow them to shed excess liquid. Drain the liquid. Add some red onion cut into small pieces, oregano and plenty of olive oil. Let the mixture marinate for half an hour. Meanwhile toast some high-quality bread – ciabatta is very good with this dish. Before you spoon the tomatoes on the bread add salt to them.

Still thinking of Calabria

These insignificant, painless, and fragmented memories
kept on emerging from somewhere deep in his mind
like bubbles that rise out of the bottom of a marsh.
Naoya Shiga

My father died in April 1976, some seven months after my son was born. It happened while we were in Rome, having proudly taken Mark to meet his wider Italian family. In the months to come, back in London, it was difficult to take in the sudden loss. I would jump whenever the telephone rang, expecting Papà's voice. Since my operation, he used to call me up almost daily, snatching a couple of minutes away from one of his building sites:

'Grazia, how are you all? And Marcolino? Is he sleeping through the night? What does he do now? Look after yourself, Grazia. *Un bacetto a Marcolino*' ('A little kiss to little Marco').

The emotional and physical involvement with Mark helped to ease the pain. Something else started happening at the same time: flashbacks. In the middle of a household or childcare task or when reading a book, I was suddenly invaded by a visual and aural scene from my early life in Delianuova. The same scene returned over and over again, prompting in me the urge to record it. I began writing down, now and then, rough notes about these scenes and anecdotes of my childhood. Once written down, that particular anecdote no longer bothered me. A different one might surface weeks or months later and leave me alone only after I had written

a brief note on it. I started a file with odd pieces of scribbled
paper. These flashbacks of my childhood life became the secret
of my mature years, just as daydreaming was my childhood and
adolescence secret. In the summer of 1978, when Donald, Mark
and I were spending our holidays at the seaside resort of Tor San
Lorenzo, I wrote a longer piece which forms the basis of the first
chapter of this book.

Cultural and geographical displacement may have played a role
in my yearning. In my 40s and 50s, time and again, while driving along the Walworth Road, a quintessential British high street,
between our home in Dulwich and my university in Elephant and
Castle, a feeling of 'disconnect', of 'not belonging', of 'what is Grazietta doing here?' came over me and often a childhood memory
resurfaced.

In the late 1990s I realized that my file 'Delianuova' had
become quite thick with a large number of scribbled pieces of paper
of all sizes. I felt a desire to organize these scribbles into a proper
memoir. Re-reading my notes I now see that those early years have
been with me ever since. In my thoughts and emotions I never left
Delianuova.

Donald and I continue to go to Rome often. Since the death of
my mother we no longer go to Tor San Lorenzo. We spend most of
our summer in London. Years ago I planted a lemon and an olive
tree in our garden. I have recently added a fig tree. I talk regularly
on the phone to my sister and brother. We exchange greetings at
Christmas and birthdays and at ... Ferragosto. In the middle of
August I am in London, Angela is in Tor San Lorenzo and Franco
is in Lipari where his wife Fiorella comes from. I ring them up.

'Franco, how are you? I hope you are having a rest. Today is
Ferragosto. Are you celebrating?

'No, Grazia, it is not a festival here in Lipari.'

'Neither in London, of course. Never mind. Buon Ferragosto to
you and Fiorella. Baci a Leonardo e Matilde!'

'Angela, Buon Ferragosto! Have you cooked the *melanzane*?'

'Yes, of course. It is not Ferragosto without *melanzane ripiene*.
Have you prepared them?'

'No. Today is not a holiday here, as you know. But I will cook them at the weekend when Marco, Deborah and the children will join us for a celebration. Penelope and Daniel love the meat filling and the small medallions I make for them. Ciao. Baci a Livia, Luca e Giulio.'

'Abbraccia Penelope e Daniel. Ciao.'

19. Grazia returns to Delianuova, 1993

Bibliography

For quotations at the beginning of chapters

Preface
Alexander Herzen, *The Pole Star*, 1855, reprinted in his *My Past and Thoughts* (Berkeley and Los Angeles: University of California Press, 1982), p. v.

Chapter 1
Dante Alighieri, *La Divina Commedia*, *Inferno*, XXIV, 46–8 (BUR, Rizzoli Editore, 1949), 132–3. English translation by John D. Sinclair, *The Divine Comedy of Dante Alighieri*, *Inferno* (London: The Bodley Head), p. 297.

Chapter 2
Alexander Pushkin, *Eugene Onegin: A Novel in Verse*, vol. I, translated by V. Nabokov (Princeton University Press, 1990), ch 1, p. 97.

Chapter 3
Erich Maria Remarque, *All Quiet on the Western Front* (London: Vintage Books, 1996 [1929]), p. 85.

Chapter 4
Collins English Dictionary (London: Collins, 1979).

Chapter 5
Alexander Pushkin, *Eugene Onegin: A Novel in Verse*, vol. I, translated by V. Nabokov (Princeton University Press, 1990), ch. 3, p. 159.

Chapter 6

Virginia Woolf, *The Waves* (Penguin Modern Classics, 1964 [1931]), p. 57.

Chapter 7

Henrik Ibsen, *The Master Builder*, in *The Master Builder and Other Plays* (Penguin Books, 1975 [1892]), p. 140.

Chapter 8

Gabriel Garcia Marquez, *One Hundred Years of Solitude* (Penguin, 1967 [1970]), p. 175.

Chapter 9

James Joyce, 'The Dead', in *Dubliners* (London: Flamingo, 1994 [1914]), pp. 203, 224.

Chapter 10

Luigi Pirandello, *Come tu mi vuoi*, Atto I (1930), from L. Pirandello, *Così è (Se vi pare)*; *Il giuoco delle parti*; *Come tu mi vuoi* (Milano: Garzanti editore, 2007), p. 170. Translation of passage by GIG.

Chapter 11

Anna Akhmatova, 'To my city', from *Selected Poems*, translated by D.M. Thomas (London, Penguin), p. 131, vv. 728-30.

Chapter 12

Salvatore Quasimodo, *Ed è subito sera*, *Di fresca donna riversa in mezzo ai fiori* (Milano: Mondadori ed, 1991 [1942]), pp. 87-8. Translation of passage from Carlo Luigi Golino, *Contemporary Italian Poetry* (Greenwood Press), p. 182.

Chapter 13

George Eliot, *The Mill on the Floss* (London: Pan Books Ltd, 1973 [1860]), p. 88.

Chapter 14

Anton Chekhov, *Five Plays: Uncle Vanya*, Act I, Dr Astrov (Oxford: OUP), p. 120.

Chapter 15

Natalia Ginzburg, *Le voci della sera* (Torino: Einaudi Editore, 2013 [1961]), p. 96. Translation by D.M.L., *Voices in the Evening* (Manchester: Carcanet Press Ltd, 1990), p. 161.

Chapter 16

Maya Angelou, *I Know Why the Caged Bird Sings* (London: Virago, 1984 [1969]), p. 221.

Chapter 17

John Keats, *The Eve of St. Agnes*, VI

George Eliot, *The Mill on the Floss* (London: Pan Books Ltd, 1973 [1860]), pp. 34-5.

Chapter 18

Harold Macmillan, July 1957.

Chapter 19

Marcel Proust, *À la recherche du temps perdu [Remembrance of Things Past]*, Part One, *Within A Budding Grove*, translated by C.K. Scott Moncrieff (London: Chatto & Windus, 1960), p. 40.

Chapter 20

Leonardo Sciascia, *Il giorno della civetta* (Einaudi, 1961), p. 32; Leonardo Sciascia, *The Day of the Owl* (Granta Books, 2001), p. 33.

Chapter 21

Gwen Raverat, *Period Piece: A Cambridge Childhood* (London: Faber and Faber, 1987 [1952]), p. 46.

Chapter 22

Maxim Gorky, *My Childhood* (Penguin Books, 1966), p. 13.

Chapter 23

George Gissing, *By the Ionian Sea. Notes of a Ramble in Southern Italy* (Oxford: Signal Books, 2004 [1901], p. 128.

Chapter 24

Ippolito Nievo, *Le Confessioni di un Italiano* (Milano: Biblioteca Universale Rizzoli, 1981 [1867]), p. 44. [*Confessions of an Italian*, translated by Frederika Randall (London: Penguin Books, 2014), pp. 43-4].

Chapter 25

Naoya Shiga, *A Dark Night's Passing*, translated by Edwin McClellan (Tokyo, New York, London: Kandaska International, 1979), p. 124.

Works cited in the text

Alvaro, C., *Gente in Aspromonte* (Garzanti, 1996, [1955])
For reference in Chapter 12.

Chekhov, A., 'Man in a Case', short story in *The Kiss and Other Stories*
(London: Penguin Books, 1982 [1898]), pp. 121–33
For reference in Chapter 12, p. 128.

Chrisafis, A., 'The exam system that puts temptation in teachers' way',
Guardian, Monday, 28 October 2002
For reference in Chapter 2.

De Amicis, E., *Cuore. Libro per ragazzi* (Milano: Einaudi, 1992 [1886])
For reference in Chapter 2, *see* De Amicis, pp. 236–70.

Dickie, J., *Delizia. The Epic History of the Italians and their Food* (New
York: Free Press, 2008)
For reference in Chapter 5 (recipes, *Salsa di pomodoro*), *see* Dickie,
Chapter 9, p. 162.
For reference in Chapter 5 (recipes, *Cooking pasta*), *see* Dickie, Chapter
12, p. 213.

Dickie, J., *Mafia Republic. Cosa Nostra, 'Ndrangheta, Camorra. 1946 to
the Present* (London: Sceptre, 2013)
For reference in Chapter 20, *see* Dickie, pp. 455–65 and p. 343.
For reference in Chapter 22, *see* Dickie, pp. 166–83.

Douglas, N., *Old Calabria* (London and New York: Tauris Parke
Paperbacks, 2010 [1915])
For reference in the Preface, *see* Douglas, pp. 281–2.
For reference in Chapter 3, *see* Douglas, Chapter 30.
The aphorism in Chapter 3, p. 25, is reported by John Davenport in
his *Introduction* to *Old Calabria*, p. 15.
For reference in Chapter 4 , *see* Douglas, Chapter 30.
For reference in Chapter 7, *see* Douglas, Chapter 31.
For reference in Chapter 7 (recipes section), *see* Douglas, Chapter 8.
For reference in Chapter 11, *see* Douglas, Chapter 15.
For reference in Chapter 19, *see* Douglas, Chapter 37.

For reference in Chapter 23, *see* Douglas, Chapter 29.

Giovene, A., *L'Autobiografia di Giuliano di Sansevero* (Roma: Elliot, 2012; English edition by Quartet Books (vols 1 and 2), translated by B. Walls)
For reference in Chapter 12.

Gissing, G., *By the Ionian Sea: Notes of a Ramble in Southern Italy* (Oxford: Signal Books, 2004 [1901])
For reference in the Preface, *see* Gissing, pp. 48–9.
For reference in Chapter 11, *see* Gissing, Chapter 13, p. 98.
For first reference in Chapter 12, *see* Gissing, Chapter 2.
For second reference in Chapter 12, *see* Gissing, Chapter 6, p. 37.
For reference in Chapter 23, *see* Gissing, Chapter 18, p. 128.

Gramsci, A., *L'albero del Riccio* (Ghilarza (OR): ISKRA Edizioni, 2002)
For reference in Chapter 9, *see* Gramsci, Lettera LI, p. 147.

Haid, K., *Calabria: The Other Italy* (Minneapolis: Mill City Press, Inc., 2015)
For reference in Chapter 11, *see* Haid, pp. 12–14.

Langley, L. 'Calabria: meeting my heroes, the superb Riace bronzes', *Daily Telegraph* (2012), http://www.telegraph.co.uk/travel/destinations/europe/italy/9254767/Calabria-meeting-my-heroes-the-superb-Riace-bronzes.html
For reference in Chapter 23.

Laruffa Editore, *I Bronzi di Riace* (Testi di Roberta Schenal Pileggi; Immagini di Francesco Turano: Reggio Calabria: Laruffa Editore, 2014)

Lear, E., *Diario di un Viaggio a Piedi* (Rubbettino Editore, 2009, [1852]); English version: *Journals of a Landscape Painter in Southern Calabria* (Andesite Press, 2016)
For reference in the Preface, *see* Lear, pp. 145–54.
For reference in Chapter 9, *see* Lear's Diary for 21 August.
For reference in Chapter 20, *see* Lear's Diary for 7 August.

Lenormant, Francois: reference in Chapter 11 taken from the quotation in Placanica, Chapter 12, p. 353.

Leuzzi, R. (a cura di), *Guida Turistica di Delianuova. Paese della Pietra Verde. Porta del Parco Nazionale d'Aspromonte* (Nuove Edizioni Barbaro di Caterina di Pietro, 2009)

Lloyd, J., 'Lunch with the FT: Elisabetta Tripodi', *Financial Times*, 10 January 2014
For reference in Chapter 6.

Placanica, A., *Storia della Calabria dall'antichita' ai giorni nostri* (Roma: Donzelli Editore, 1999, [1993])
For reference in Chapter 6, *see* Placanica, II.
For reference in Chapter 12, *see* Placanica, p. 186.
For reference in Chapter 22, *see* Placanica p. 343

Raverat, Gwen, *Period Piece: A Cambridge Childhood* (London: Faber and Faber, paperback edition, 1960)
For reference in Chapter 6, *see* Raverat, p. 124

Wong, J., 'The time has come for dandelions', *Observer Magazine*, 1 May 2016, p. 49
For reference in Chapter 24.

Index of recipes

Spaghetti alle vongole (spaghetti with clams)	119–20
Stoccafissu/Baccalà (cod)	23
Tortino di acciughe e patate (anchovy and potato pie)	23

Meat dishes

Cotolette panate (breaded cutlets)	134
Meat and aubergine medallions/fritters	88
Melanzane ripiene (stuffed aubergines)	81–3
Polpettine di Zia Angelina (Zia Angelina's small meat balls)	52
Ragù	65
Scaloppine al vino o al limone (wine or lemon escalopes)	134
Stufato di pollo (chicken stew)	135

Pasta asciutta dishes: pasta to be eaten with a fork

Linguine al prezzemolo (linguine with parsley)	109
Linguine all'aglio, olio e peperoncino (linguine with garlic, oil and chilli)	109
Linguine alle acciughe (linguine with anchovy sauce)	109
Pappardelle o tagliatelle ai funghi porcini (pappardelle or tagliatelle with ceps)	120
Pasta al forno (baked pasta)	65–6
Pasta alla Napoletana	65
Pasta con ragù	65
Pasta e ricotta	13–14
Pasta with asparagus	118
Penne all'arrabbiata (penne in … an angry mood)	66
Spaghetti al pomodoro fresco (spaghetti with fresh tomato)	119
Spaghetti al tonno (spaghetti with tuna)	119
Spaghetti alle vongole (spaghetti with clams)	119–20
Spaghetti/linguine con zucchine (spaghetti or linguine with courgettes)	118

Rice dishes

Pomodori col riso (tomatoes stuffed with rice)	145–6
Rice salad	146–7

Soups, thick

Soups, thin

Vegetables